100 Years
100 Songs

OMNIBUS PRESS

London · New York · Paris · Sydney · Copenhagen · Madrid · Tokyo

Music compiled by Peter Evans
and Philip Glassborow.
Music arranged by Derek Jones.
Music processed by Paul Ewers Music Design.

Edited by Chris Charlesworth.
Background notes by Philip Glassborow (1900-49)
and Rikky Rooksby (1950-99).
Introduction by Philip Glassborow.

Book designed by Pearce Marchbank, Studio Twenty, London.

Pictures and captions edited by Pearce Marchbank.
Picture research by Nikki Lloyd and Lisa Quas.

All photographs courtesy of
The Hulton Getty Picture Collection Limited,
except the following which are courtesy of...
Rex Features Ltd: 14, 16, 136, 166, 168, 170, 171,174 178, 181,
192 194, 195, 196, 198, 200, 205, 206, 209, 212, 216, 218,
220, 223, 224, 229, 230, 232, 233, 234, 236.
Corbis: 9, 46, 60, 131, 158, 162.
The Kobal Collection: 6, 56, 72, 120, 153.
London Features International: 132, 188, 214.
Redferns: 106, 140, 177, 182.
Digital Vision: 174, 230.
Daily Mail: 238.

Exclusive Distributors:
Book Sales Limited
8-9 Frith Street,
London W1V 5TZ.
Music Sales Pty Limited
120 Rothschild Avenue,
Rosebery NSW 2018,
Australia.

ISBN 0-7119-7909-X

Printed in the United Kingdom by
Caligraving Limited, Thetford, Norfolk.

Your Guarantee of Quality
As publishers, we strive to produce every book to the
highest commercial standards.
The music has been freshly engraved and the book has been
carefully designed to minimise awkward page turns and to make
playing from it a real pleasure.
Throughout, the printing and binding have been planned to
ensure a sturdy, attractive publication which should give years of
enjoyment. If your copy fails to meet our high standards,
please inform us and we will gladly replace it.

www.omnibuspress.com

One of the many cabaret
acts of the Twenties,
The Dodge Twins
pictured at the height of
the decade's androgynous
'flapper' fashions.

These are the songs that define the decades, the tunes that evoke their times and also transcend time. Simply glance at the list of song titles, and you're singing. It's quite amazing how many of these songs are instantly familiar to us. But how did all that music get into our heads?

There has always been music in the air. Nowadays, it may be muzak in the mall, to stimulate our shopping, or elevator music, specially synthesised to soothe away our stress. But in a gentler age, the tunes were played live by a Palm Court Orchestra in the grander hotels, or a romantic gypsy band in more raffish restaurants. Even in the unsalubrious Storyville houses of ill repute, a piano player was generally on hand to add a touch of class. ("Don't shoot the pianist!")

Yet in those long-lost days, automation was not unknown. Turn-of-the-century street musicians had all manner of ingenious devices to help fill the air with tunes, such as the hurdy-gurdy or barrel-organ. (Today's buskers are simply making use of the modern equivalents, when they play along to pre-recorded backing tracks.)

"Melodies bring memories that linger in my heart"
'Georgia On My Mind'

So, how did the popular songs become popular in the first place? Songs "happen" in a variety of ways. As the century began, most new songs were introduced to the public through live performances in the theatre, the concert hall or the music hall. If a song caught on and became a hit, it sold thousands of copies of sheet music. (Patrons could even purchase their songsheets from the theatre attendants on the way out – hence the phrase "a take-home song".) Many homes had pianos, and so the songs truly became an integral part of people's lives: they experienced the music by actually playing or singing their favourite numbers, over and over again.

As the media developed, songs were introduced on radio, in films, and on TV. Hits were progressively defined by sales of piano-rolls (for mechanical player-pianos), wax cylinders, 78rpm discs, 45rpm singles, 33rpm albums, cartridges, pre-recorded cassettes, CDs, mini-discs and many other "sound-carriers".

Today, a song might become popular through exposure in a blockbuster movie like *Titanic*, or from its use in a TV commercial. But the real-live experience of music still registers very strongly on sales, which is why so many bands continue to tour and play concerts as a means of promoting their albums.

And although the rhythms have changed (from ragtime, to rock'n'roll, to reggae and rap, and beyond) some things have remained constant. We, the people, still love songs, and consume them voraciously. There's nothing like a hit!

Once established as a hit, a song becomes a hardy perennial, but on its way to full flower, any song is vulnerable to a thousand blights and vagaries. 'Over The Rainbow' is part of the soundtrack to almost everyone's life, but it was nearly cut from *The Wizard Of Oz*, and might have withered away in oblivion on the cutting-room floor. Paul McCartney's 'Yesterday' (its working title was 'Scrambled Eggs') was originally scoffed at by the other three Beatles, yet it now has the distinction of being the most-recorded song of all time. You will find out more about both songs in the pages of this book.

Popular songs are often a meaningful part of our own history ("They're playing our song"). Songs can be part of social history – the restless Charleston rhythms of the twenties help to define their era. Indeed, songs can even make history. Message songs like Bob Dylan's 'Blowin' In The Wind' or John Lennon's 'Give Peace A Chance' (both of which can be found in these pages) undeniably had an impact on the zeitgeist of their day. ▷

"Song is the joint art of words and music, two arts under emotional pressure coalescing into a third."
Encyclopaedia Britannica

Marlene Dietrich in 1930, the year she recorded 'Falling In Love Again'.

"Moonlight and love songs, never out of date"
'As Time Goes By'

As Richard Rodgers once said, "A song is the voice of its times." And what can evoke the psychedelic Sixties better than 'Strawberry Fields Forever'? If one picture is worth a thousand words, then surely a song speaks volumes. And if all songs say something about their times, the finest songs do something more – they speak for all time. The great 'standards' keep coming back like a song, to be rediscovered afresh by new generations.

If you first heard 'Try A Little Tenderness' in the movie *The Commitments*, or performed by Michael Bolton or Rod Stewart, then you may not know Otis Redding's classic version from 1967. Yet the song itself actually dates all the way back to 1933.

A retrospective like this gives us the opportunity to explore which songs have made a lasting impression over the decades. Some great songs were overlooked initially, but later found popularity. 'As Time Goes By' didn't set the world on fire when it was first introduced in a Broadway stage revue, but several years later, it found its way to immortality in the movie *Casablanca*.

Other songs were acclaimed in their time but have faded from view. Nominations for the Best Song Oscar of 1937 included 'They Can't Take That Away From Me' and 'That Old Feeling', both of which instantly become standards. But the winner that year was 'Sweet Leilani', which, although a delightful song, is rarely if ever heard today.

The Selection

"It was the best of times, it was the worst of times" by which I mean, not the twentieth century, but the agonising process of selecting one hundred of its most significant songs.

Only a hundred! Trying to keep the list down to a mere thousand essential standards would have been hard enough. But just 100 songs to represent 100 of the most eventful and song-packed years in history? I ask you.

Mind you, the terms of reference certainly helped to narrow the field. Each song must have been a hit in its day. And furthermore, each song must serve as a landmark, because of its impact at the time, or its writers, or its best-known performers, or a particular genre which it represents.

The editors could have compiled this book in many ways. *A Century of Great Singers* would have spotlighted the key songs of such performers of their time as Elvis Presley, Bing Crosby, The Beatles and The Spice Girls. *A Century of Tin Pan Alley* would have highlighted the great popular songwriters of the songs of the century. *A Century of Movie Music*... well, you take the point. (Anyway, the publishers have recently produced an excellent book of that title, which is now available in all good music stores.)

Instead, the editors compiled one volume – the book you hold in your hands right now – combining the most significant popular songs of the century, whether from Tin Pan Alley or Hollywood, Liverpool or Sweden or Nashville or Barbados. Every song included here was voted for, argued for and passionately defended, in a smoke-filled room, as the debate about the final selection raged into the small hours. Some of your personal favourites may be missing, as are some of mine, but among the hundred songs selected to represent the century, there will doubtless be many that you approve.

The music editors have presented each song in an ingenious condensed melody-line arrangement, eminently playable on keyboard or any 'C' instrument, along with chord names, and of course the lyrics, which are complete wherever practicable. ▷

December, 1943: The cutting-edge in zoot suits, Harlem, New York.

The Lyrics

Songs are documents of their times, and so, when judged by today's more enlightened standards, the lyrics of many older songs can now seem deeply offensive. Yet when they are great songs, like 'Ol' Man River', it would be foolhardy to alter the words to fit our contemporary sensibilities. The songs are themselves valuable historical documents, and, sadly, we cannot rewrite history by retrospectively editing song lyrics.

Please, therefore, try to make allowances for the lyric-writers of another time if anything here offends your eye. The past is another country. And remember, also, the context of the songs. A cold reading of the lyrics "Colored folks work on de Mississippi, Colored folks work while de white folks play" is shocking, but it's important to remember that the song was written for a character in a play, with a particular dramatic agenda, and that the lyricist, Oscar Hammerstein II, was not condoning racism. In fact, he later wrote a very clever song condemning racism – 'You've Got To Be Carefully Taught' from *South Pacific*.

The Notes

Editorial notes are included for each song, and the notes on the songs from 1899 to 1949 are very different in style to the notes from 1950 to the end of the century. This is because the songs from the first half of the century are considered primarily as songs, while songs from 1950 onwards are discussed more in terms of their best-known recordings.

In the century's earlier years, a song would be performed and even recorded by many different artists. In time, an oft-performed and much-covered song would become that most precious commodity, a 'standard'. This still happens from time to time, but these days we tend to associate a hit song with one particular, definitive recording.

So, in the notes for every song from 1950 onwards, a chart position is included. The charts were not particularly relevant during the first half of the century, but we do occasionally mention significant chart positions, even for songs of a much earlier vintage. ▷

Celebrating V-E Day
(Victory In Europe Day)
in a street off Whitehall,
London, 1945.

The Charts

Billboard's weekly charts began in 1940, and Britain's *Melody Maker* followed the US listings for several years before the UK's own official charts began. Even before then, other "Hit Parade" listings were available from sundry sources. Some of the first charts were based on sheet music sales, although *Variety* magazine was printing monthly rankings of best-selling records by the late nineteen-twenties. Very early sales figures of gramophone records and cylinders were also printed in a long-vanished magazine called *Talking Machine World.* Joel Whitburn's excellent book *Pop Memories 1890-1954* collates these many-and-various listings, and has now become the accepted standard for vintage "charts". So when we quote pre-1950 chart positions, we refer to Whitburn.

Other source-books we have found of immeasurable help, and which we acknowledge with gratitude: *Tin Pan Alley: The Composers, The Songs, The Performers and Their Times* by David A. Jasen (Omnibus Press, 1990); *The Complete Encyclopaedia of Popular Music and Jazz, 1900-1950 by Roger D. Kinkle* (Arlington House Publishers, 1974); *Lives of the Great Songs,* edited by Tim de Lisle (Pavilion Books, 1994): *The Guinness Book Of Hit Singles,* various editions and authors.

A final thought, dear reader. When considering the one hundred landmark songs in this magnificent collection, remember that they were written to be listened to, played and sung. So...enjoy! Sing! Play! Make a joyful noise...
Philip Glassborow.

Double Fantasy
Yoko
Contains the Hit Song:
(Just Like)
Starting Over

December, 1980: Outside John Lennon's home with Yoko Ono in the Dakota Building in New York City, tributes pile-up from mourning fans after his shooting there.

A candle in the wind...
Princess Diana dancing
on stage at a Royal Ballet
gala (see page 192).

At the birth of the century, an early airship drifts unseen over a busy south London street.

I'll Be Your Sweetheart
1899

At the turn of the century, 'I'll Be Your Sweetheart' was a resounding hit for songwriter Harry Dacre, following his international success with 'Daisy Bell (A Bicycle Made for Two)'. Thanks to its lilting chorus in waltz time, this delightful number, nostalgically scented with essence of bluebells, has proved an enduring favourite among barbershop quartets and parlour singers. Other elegant hit songs of the year included 'Tell Me Pretty Maiden' (from the stage show *Floradora*) and 'A Bird In A Gilded Cage'.

I'll Be Your Sweetheart

Words & Music by Harry Dacre

Verse 2:
The blue bells were accepted by the maiden
She said "I'll keep them safely all my life.
But then suppose you meet some other lady
And I should never be your darling wife"
He shook his head and took another kiss
Then once again he whispered this:

Verse 3:
The years flew by and once again I saw them
They stood before the altar hand in hand.
A handsome pair, I never shall forget them
The happiest couple in the land.
And once again he took the loving kiss
Then passionately whispered this:

Land Of Hope And Glory
(Pomp And Circumstance March No.1)

Music by Sir Edward Elgar
Words by Arthur Benson

Majestically

Land of hope and glo - - - ry,
Moth - er of the Free, how shall we ex -
- tol thee who are born of thee?
Wi - der still and wi - der shall thy bounds be
set; God, who made thee migh - ty,
make thee migh - tier yet. God, who made thee
migh - - ty, make thee migh - tier yet.

Land Of Hope And Glory
1902

"I've got a tune that will knock 'em – knock 'em flat" wrote Edward Elgar to a friend. He used the "knock 'em flat" tune as the first of his *Pomp And Circumstance* marches in 1901, where it was much admired, notably by Prince (soon to be King) Edward. Elgar promptly adapted the tune to fit words specially written by A. C. Benson to celebrate the coronation of Edward VII in 1902. It was first performed by the great Dame Clara Butt, and has been a firm favourite of British audiences ever since. It is lustily sung each year by the entire audience of the Albert Hall at the Last Night of the Proms, and has often been proposed as an alternative National Anthem for the United Kingdom.

One of the last official portraits taken of the old Queen Victoria, just months before her death in 1902.

Bill Bailey Won't You Please Come Home

Words & Music by Hughie Cannon

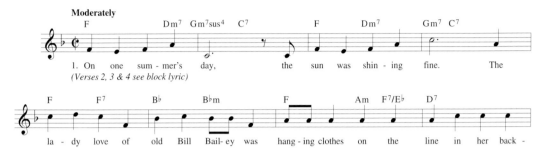

Moderately

1. On one sum - mer's day, the sun was shin - ing fine. The
(Verses 2, 3 & 4 see block lyric)

la - dy love of old Bill Bail- ey was hang - ing clothes on the line in her back -

Bill Bailey Won't You Please Come Home *1902*
By way of total contrast with Elgar's stately march, another hit of 1902 was 'Bill Bailey Won't You Please Come Home'. Hughie Cannon's joyous syncopated ragtime song was reputedly inspired by an incident in real life, and several candidates have been suggested for the original "Bill Bailey". The song also inspired a number of sequels speculating about what might have happened when Bill Bailey finally did come home.

Music Hall was king. With no TV, radio, cinema, records... it was the people's only choice for entertainment outside the home.

Verse 2:
She wed a B.N.O brakeman
That went and threw her down.
Hollering like a prune-fed calf
With a big gang hanging round
And to that crowd she'd yell out loud.

Verse 3:
Bill drove by that door
In an automobile.
A great big diamond coach and footmen
Hear that big girl squeal:
"He's all alone" I heard her groan.

Verse 4:
She hollered through that door
Bill Bailey are you sure.
Stop a minute, won't you listen
Won't I you see no more?
Bill winked his eye as he heard her cry.

Alexander's *Ragtime Band*

Words & Music by Irving Berlin

Moderately

1. Oh, ma hon-ey, oh, ma hon-ey, bet-ter hur-ry and let's me-an-der,

(Verse 2 see block lyric)

ain't you go-in', ain't you go-in', to the lead-er man, rag-ged me-ter man?

A a pre-war street band parades through New Orleans.

Alexander's Ragtime Band *1911*

'Alexander's Ragtime Band' was the first smash hit for Irving Berlin, who went on to create an astonishing catalogue of all-time standards, despite the fact that he only played the piano in one key – F sharp – and could neither read nor write music notation. (Musical purists will note that the most famous of all "ragtime" songs isn't actually written in ragtime!) *Alexander's Ragtime Band* was also the title of a 1938 musical movie from 20th Century Fox, featuring no less that 32 of Berlin's songs.

From his many hundreds of standard hits, a tiny sampling: 'There's No Business Like Show Business' (the unofficial anthem of the entertainment industry), 'God Bless America', 'Blue Skies', 'Let's Face The Music And Dance', and of course 'White Christmas'.

Oh, ma hon-ey, oh, ma hon-ey let me take you to Al - ex - an - der's
grand stand, brass band, ain't you com - in' a - long?___ Come on and
hear,___ come on and hear,___ Al - ex - an - der's rag - time band,___ come on and
hear,___ come on and hear,___ it's the best band in the land,___ they can
play a bu - gle call like you nev - er heard be - fore, so nat - ur - al that you want to go to war.
that's just the best - est band that am, hon - ey lamb; come on a -
- long,___ come on a - long,___ let me take you by the hand,___ up to the
man,___ up to the man___ who's the lead - er of the band,___ and if you
care to hear the Swa - nee Riv - er played in rag - time,___ come on and
hear,___ come on and hear,___ Al - ex - an - der's rag - time band. band.

Verse 2:
Oh, ma honey, oh, ma honey
There's a fiddle with notes that screeches
Like a chicken, like a chicken
And the clarinet, is a colored pet
Come and listen, come and listen
To a classical band what's peaches
Come now, some how
Better hurry along.

Memphis Blues

Words & Music by W.C.Handy

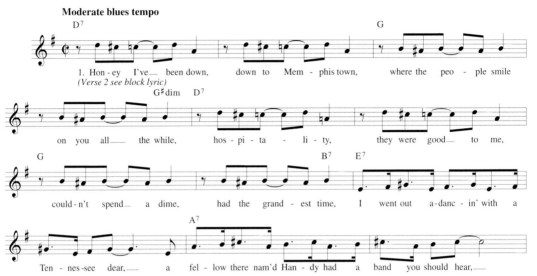

Moderate blues tempo

1. Hon - ey I've— been down, down to Mem - phis town, where the peo - ple smile
(Verse 2 see block lyric)

on you all—— the while, hos - pi - ta - li - ty, they were good— to me,

could - n't spend— a dime, had the grand - est time, I went out a - danc - in' with a

Ten - nes - see dear,— a fel - low there nam'd Han - dy had a band you should hear,——

Memphis Blues
1912
'Memphis Blues' was the first published song by "The Father of the Blues", W.C.Handy. He also composed many other blues numbers, including 'St Louis Blues', which was – until overtaken by 'Yesterday' – the most-recorded popular song of the twentieth century. Handy had been the musical director of a minstrel show, a bandmaster and teacher before becoming a songwriter and publisher. Among his pioneering publications were *Blues: An Anthology* in 1926 and an important early collection of spirituals.

April, 1912: The 'unsinkable' Titanic sails from Southampton on it's first and last voyage.

Following pages
April, 1926: An all-night ball on board the then largest liner in the world the Majestic, a later White Star Line ship, safely moored at Southampton docks.

while they gent - ly swayed, all them dark - ies played real har - mon - y. I nev - er will for - get the tune that Han - dy called the Mem-phis blues, oh, them blues. They got a fid - dler there that al - ways slick - ens his hair, oh, lor - dy, how he pulls on his bow. And when you hear that tune, lis - ten to the trom-bones croon, they moan just like a sin - ner on Re-vi - val Day, on that old Re-vi - val Day. That me - lan - cho - ly strain, that ev - er haunt - ing re - frain is like a dar - key moan - in' a song, here comes the ve - ry part that wraps a spell a-round my heart, it sets me wild to hear that love - ly tune a - gain, those Mem-phis Blues. They got a

1. **2, 3.** *D.C. al Fine* *Fine*

Verse 2:
Oh, that melody sure appeals to me
Like a mountain stream, flowing on it seem'd
Then it slowly died, with a gentle sigh
As the breeze that whines in the summer pines
Hear me people, hear me people, hear me, I pray
I'll take a million lessons till I learn how to play
Seems I hear it yet, simply can't forget, that blue refrain
There's nothing like the Handy Band
That plays the Memphis Blues so grand, oh them blues.

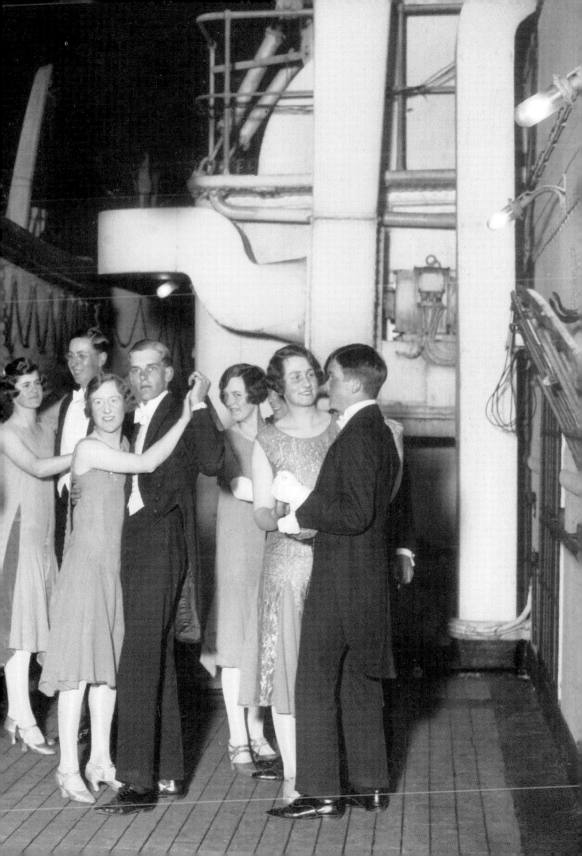

A painting for a recruiting poster from the First World War by popular American illustrator Alfred Everitt O... The banner headline read 'For Home and Country'.*

Keep The Home Fires Burning *1914*

The rallying words by Lena Guilbert Ford are set to stirring music by David Ivor Davies, better known as matinee idol, songwriter, playwright and producer Ivor Novello. He was renowned for lush, romantic musicals like *Glamorous Night* and *Perchance To Dream* (with its hit song 'We'll Gather Lilacs') but he also composed delightful art songs such as 'The Little Damozel' and witty revue numbers like 'And Her Mother Came Too'.

Keep The Home Fires Burning

Music by Ivor Novello
Words by Lena Guilbert-Ford

March

1. They were sum-moned from the hill - side, they were called in from the glen. And the
(Verse 2 see block lyric)
coun - try found them read - y at the stir - ing call for men. Let no
tears add to their hard - ship, as the sol - diers pass a - long. And al - though your heart is
break - ing, make it sing this cheer - y song. Keep the home fires burn - ing, while your hearts are yearn - ing. Though your lads are far a - way, they dream of home. There's a sil - ver lin - ing, through the dark cloud shin - ing. Turn the dark cloud

1. in - side out till the boys come home.
2. home.

Verse 2:
Over seas there came a pleading
"Help a Nation in distress!"
And we gave our glorious laddies
Honour bade us do no less.
For no gallant Son of Britain
To a foreign yoke shall bend
And no Englishman is silent
To the sacred call of Friend.

They Didn't Believe Me

Music by Jerome Kern
Words by Herbert Reynolds

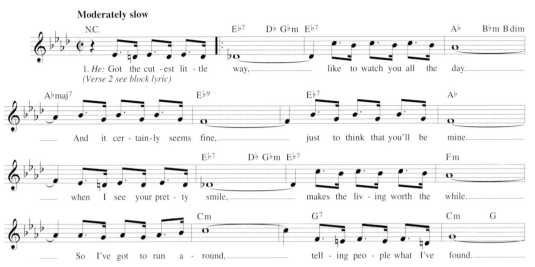

Moderately slow

1. *He:* Got the cut-est lit-tle way, like to watch you all the day.
(*Verse 2 see block lyric*)

And it cer-tain-ly seems fine, just to think that you'll be mine.

when I see your pret-ty smile, makes the liv-ing worth the while.

So I've got to run a-round, tell-ing peo-ple what I've found.

They Didn't Believe Me
1914
Jerome Kern's first big hit became a significant song during the Great War, partly through its ironic rendition by the soldiers, as seen in the stage show and movie *Oh! What A Lovely War.*

American officers brush-up their French for the expected entry into "gay Paree" towards the end of the First World War.

Slowly

And when I told them how beau-ti-ful you are, they did-n't be-

lieve me, they did-n't be-lieve me! Your lips, your eyes, your cheeks, your

hair are in a class be-yond com-pare. You're the lov-li-est girl that one could

see! And when I tell them, and I cert'n-ly am goin' to

tell them, that I'm the man whose wife one day you'll

be, they'll ne-ver be-lieve me, they'll ne-ver be-

lieve me. That from this great big world you've cho-sen

1. me! 2. *She:* Don't know how it hap-pened me!

2.

Verse 2:
She:
Don't know how it happened quite
May have been the summer night
May have been, well who can say
Things just happen any way.
All I know is I said "Yes!"
Hesitating more or less
And you kissed me where I stood
Just like any fellow would.

And when I told them
How wonderful you are
They didn't believe me
They didn't believe me!
Your lips, your eyes, your curly hair
Are in a class beyond compare.
You're the loveliest thing
That one could see!

And when I tell them
And I certainly am goin' to tell them
That I'm the girl whose boy
One day you'll be.
They'll never believe me
They'll never believe me
That from this great big world
You've chosen me!

Swanee *1919*

'Swanee' was the first important hit song for a young composer called George Gershwin. The year before his first Broadway show opened (*La La Lucille*), he was asked to write this number for the opening of the Capitol Theatre on Broadway. Then Al Jolson interpolated the song in the musical *Sinbad* (it was a natural for Jolie, with its pulsing, powerhouse refrain 'Swanee, how I love you, how I love you' and its mentions of Mammy and the old folks at home) and it became the biggest sheet music hit of Gershwin's entire career. For more on Al Jolson, see 'The Anniversary Song', also in this collection.

The lyrics for 'Swanee' were by Irving Caesar, whose other famous songs include 'Tea For Two', 'Is It True What They Say About Dixie', 'I Want To Be Happy' and 'Animal Crackers' for Shirley Temple.

Al Jolson changing into his alternative stage persona as he blacks-up in his dressing room.

Swanee

Music & Lyrics by George Gershwin & Irving Caesar

Fascinating Rhythm

Music & Lyrics by George Gershwin & Ira Gershwin

In the 1920's the rhythm of New York's skyline was taking shape. As they were famous for their lack of fear of heights, many of the construction workers were native American Indians.

Fascinating Rhythm

1924

Long before Fred and Ginger, it was Fred and Adele. Brother and sister Astaire were the scintillating stars of such Broadway shows as *Lady Be Good* (in which they introduced this evergreen standard), *Funny Face* and *The Band Wagon*. They also proved such a wow in London that they were taken up by the smart set of the Twenties, and even by royalty. When Adele retired from the stage to become Lady Cavendish, it was feared that Fred would never again find so perfect a partner.

However, despite the discouraging verdict on his first screen test for Hollywood... "Can't act. Slightly bald. Can dance a little"...he went on to even greater international success when he teamed up with Ginger Rogers. See also 'The Way You Look Tonight'.

If You Knew Susie *1925*

This peppy number – with its catchy "Oh, Oh, Oh, What A Girl!" refrain – was perfect for the energetic, knock-em-dead delivery of stars like Al Jolson and Eddie Cantor. Clearly, the singer is enthusiastically smitten with Susie (she does sound like quite a girl) and the song belongs with other high-energy numbers like 'Yes, Sir, That's My Baby' from the same year and 'I'm Just Wild About Harry' from 1922.

'If You Knew Susie' sold over a million copies of sheet music, and later became the title of an Eddie Cantor movie. Songwriters Joseph Meyer and B. G. "Buddy" De Sylva were also responsible for hits like 'California, Here I Come'. Buddy De Sylva wrote with George Gershwin ('Somebody Loves Me'), Jerome Kern ('Look For The Silver Lining') and most notably was part of the famous trio Ray Henderson, Buddy De Sylva and Lew Brown ('Sonny Boy', 'Button Up Your Overcoat', 'If I Had A Talking Picture Of You'). He later became a producer of several Shirley Temple films and Broadway shows, and eventually head of Paramount Pictures. De Sylva was one of the three founders of Capitol Records in 1942 (with Glenn Wallichs and fellow songwriter Johnny Mercer).

If You Knew Susie

Words & Music by Buddy De Sylva & Joseph Meyer

Brightly

1. If you knew Su - sie, like I know Su - sie,

(Verse 2 see block lyric)

oh, oh, oh what a girl! There's

none so clas - sy as this fair las - sie,

oh, oh! Ho - ly Mo - ses, what a chas - sis!

We went rid - ing, she did - n't balk.

Back from Yon - kers, I'm the one who had to walk! If

you knew Su - sie, like I know Su - sie,

1.
oh, oh what a girl! 2. If

2.

Verse 2:
If you knew Susie, like I know Susie
Oh, oh, oh what a girl!
She wears long tresses and nice tight dresses
Oh, oh! What a future she possesses!
Out in public how she can yawn
In a parlor, you would think the war was on!
If you knew Susie, like I know Susie
Oh, oh what a girl!

Show Me The Way To Go Home

Words & Music by Irving King & Hal Swain

Moderately

1. When I'm hap - py, when I'm hap - py, sing - ing all the while,
(Verse 2 see block lyric)

I don't need no - bo - dy then to show me how to smile.

When I've been out on the spree, tod - dling down the street,

with this lit - tle me - lo - dy ev - ery - one I greet.

Show me the way to go home, I'm tired and I want to go to bed. I

had a lit tle drink a - bout an hour a - go and it's gone right to my head. Where

ev - er I may roam, on land or sea or foam, you can al - ways hear me

sing - ing this song, show me the way to go home. home.

Verse 2:
Old King Cole was a merry old soul
And a merry old soul was he
He called for his wine and he called for his pipe
And he called for his fiddlers three.
When they'd had a high old time
All the whole night through
What was it that King Cole said
And his fiddlers too?

At the height of Prohibition, following a raid on a Chicago warehouse, illegal alcohol is zealously destroyed by government agents.

Show Me The Way To Go Home *1925*

Jimmy Campbell and Reg Connelly knew it would be a smash hit. But the two songwriters couldn't find anyone in London to publish it. So they set up their own music publishing company. And within a few weeks, their song was indeed a sensational success, featured by the bandleader at the Savoy and selling thousands of copies of sheet music. The song was 'Show Me The Way To Go Home', and the writers were Jimmy Campbell and Reg Connelly (using the pseudonym Irving King, because they also appeared on the music cover as Campbell Connelly & Co. Limited) and Hal Swain. Later the same year, they published a surprisingly racy follow-up number entitled 'She Showed Him This – She Showed Him That – She Showed Him The Way To Go Home'.

Airships were the great air travel hope of the Twenties. But after the crashes of both the hydrogen filled German Hindenberg and the British R101 (seen here docking at its home base near Bedford) the public saw them as too dangerous.

Bye Bye Blackbird *1926*
In the swinging Sixties, the instrument of choice for most young people was a guitar. But way back in the roaring Twenties, the Bright Young Things and the college kids were crazy about the ukelele. It was relatively cheap, kind of easy, and best of all, wondrously portable. Sure, you could get music from the wind-up gramophone (wax cylinders were by now passé) or – occasionally – from the wireless.

But in those far-off yesterdays, music was very much home-made. And what could be a better way to serenade a sweetie, or lead a convivial sing-song, than with a handy ukelele? Performers like Cliff "Ukelele Ike" Edwards (see 'It's Only A Paper Moon' on page 72) and even the animated cartoon star, Elmo Aardvark, helped to popularise the trend.

An all-time favourite among the ukelele fraternity was 'Bye Bye Blackbird'. The music was

by Ray Henderson, of the fabled Henderson-De Sylva-Brown songwriting team (mentioned in the note on 'If You Knew Susie'). The words were by Mort Dixon, whose other hits included 'I'm Looking Over A Four Leaf Clover', 'Would You Like To Take A Walk', and 'I Found A Million Dollar Baby (In A Five And Ten Cent Store)'.

Bye Bye Blackbird

Words by Mort Dixon
Music by Ray Henderson

Moderately

Pack up all my care and woe, here I go, sing - ing low.

Bye bye black - bird.

Where some - bo - dy waits for me, su - gar's sweet, so is she.

Bye bye black - bird.

No one here can love and un - der - stand me,

oh what hard luck sto - ries they all hand me.

Make my bed and light the light, I'll ar - rive late to - night.

1. Black - bird bye bye.

2. bye.

Ol' Man River

Music by Jerome Kern
Words by Oscar Hammerstein II

Ol' Man River *1927*

This magnificent number was only one of the many hit songs from *Show Boat*, the musical that revolutionised American theatre. The song was written for Paul Robeson, although he didn't appear in *Show Boat* until the London premiere in 1928 and the first major musical film version in 1936. It was his superb 1925 concert of spirituals which inspired Kern to write 'Ol' Man River'.

Edna Ferber, author of the novel on which the musical was based, describes her response on first hearing the melody...

"Jerome Kern appeared at my apartment late one afternoon with a strange look of quiet exaltation in his eyes. He sat down at the piano. He didn't play the piano particularly well, and his singing voice, though true, was negligible. He played and sang 'Ol' Man River'. The music mounted, mounted, and I give you my word my hair stood on end, the tears came to my eyes. This was great music. This was music that would outlast Jerome Kern's day and mine."

But what makes a great song? When the right words find the right music. Legend has it that the wives of composer Jerome Kern and lyricist Oscar Hammerstein II both happened to be at a Hollywood party. Mrs Kern was explaining to another guest that her husband had written 'Ol' Man River'. "Oh, no," said Mrs Hammerstein, "my husband wrote 'Ol' Man River'. Your husband wrote 'La-la-la-la'."

Another dance marathon starts at Coney Island in 1928. Most entered only in a desperate attempt to win the large prize money, as shown in the play and film They Shoot Horses Don't They?

I Can't Give You Anything But Love *1928*
Composer Jimmy McHugh collaborated with Dorothy Fields on this sassy number and many other hits like 'On The Sunny Side Of The Street', 'I'm In The Mood For Love', 'Exactly Like You' and 'Dinner At Eight'.

Following pages June, 1926: The latest London night spot is the 'Thames-side resort' The Palm Beach ballroom and cabaret.

I Can't Give You Anything But Love

Words by Dorothy Fields
Music by Jimmy McHugh

Sweet Sue-Just You

Words by Will J. Harris
Music by Victor Young

Verse 2:
Why, should you sit around and sigh
When the sun up in the sky shines for you and I?
My Sue, I have always loved you
Now that you know it, to show it, I'll try.

Regardless of the General Strike and the depression, London's partying classes continued as normal.

Sweet Sue-Just You *1928* This jaunty song became a hit for many artists, ranging from The Mills Brothers to bandleader Tommy Dorsey, the Sentimental Gentleman of Swing. The lyrics are by Will J. Harris, and the music is by Victor Young, whose many other hits and film songs include 'When I Fall In Love' and 'Around The World In Eighty Days'. (A popular name in popular song, Susan turns up again in 'If You Knew Susie' on page 38).

Fats Waller was a brilliant stride piano player and a fine songwriter. His vivacious recordings made him a major popular entertainer.

Ain't Misbehavin' *1929*

'Ain't Misbehavin'' boasted music by Thomas Waller (better known as Fats) and words by the lyricist of 'Honeysuckle Rose', 'Black And Blue', 'Memories Of You' and many other hit songs. He was an African Prince, born to African Royal parents, and a grand-nephew of the Queen of Madagascar. His full name was Andrea Razafkeriefo, but on Tin Pan Alley, they called him Andy Razaf.

Exuberant Fats Waller performed and wrote some of the happiest jazz ever recorded. He scored a special hit with this number, which also became his theme song. Fats performed it in the 1943 musical movie *Stormy Weather* and also recorded it several times. One of his recordings has been retrospectively honoured by the National Academy of Recording Arts and Sciences (the Grammy Awards organisation) and placed in the NARAS Hall of Fame.

Ain't Misbehavin'

Words by Andy Razaf
Music by Thomas 'Fats' Waller & Harry Brooks

Moderately

Body And Soul

Music by John Green
Lyrics by Frank Eyton, Edward Heyman & Robert Sour

Expressively

My heart is sad and lone - ly, for you I sigh, for you dear, on - ly. Why have - n't you seen it? I'm all for you, bo - dy and soul! I spend my days in long - ing and won - d'ring why it's me you're wrong - ing. I tell you I mean it, I'm all for you, bo - dy and soul. I can't be - lieve it, it's hard to con - ceive it, that you'd turn a - way ro - mance. Are you pre - tend - ing, it looks like the end - ing, un - less I could have one more dance to prove dear. My life a wreck you're mak - ing, you know I'm yours for just the tak - ing; I'd glad - ly sur - ren - der my - self to you, bo - dy and soul! soul!

Gertrude Lawrence with Noël Coward at the first performance of his ghost comedy Blythe Spirit.

Body And Soul *1930*
Composed by John Green, whose other song hits include 'Coquette', 'I Cover The Waterfront', 'Easy Come, Easy Go' and 'Out Of Nowhere'. The British star Gertrude Lawrence asked Green to write a batch of four songs for her cabaret appearances. Three are now forgotten, but the "torch song" became his most enduring hit. When he was later asked by an interviewer if he knew at the time that he was writing a classic, he replied, "I only knew it had to be ready by Wednesday." It remains one of the most often-recorded songs of all time, especially by jazz musicians, who admire its chord structure and haunting progressions. The classic Coleman Hawkins version of 1940 was one of the eight inaugural recordings to be retrospectively placed in the NARAS Hall of Fame.

Falling In Love Again *1930*
Marlene Dietrich shot to
international stardom in the
landmark German film, *The Blue
Angel.* Listen, if you can, to her
original recording of this song,
and you'll hear a pretty, almost
sweet voice in the higher
register, playful and girlish –
especially in the German-
language version – and entirely
without the world-weary

huskiness that later came to
characterise her vocal
performances. The haunting
waltz remained Marlene's
signature song for the rest of her
long and starry career.
The composer was Frederick
Hollander, who, like Dietrich,
was snapped up by Hollywood
following the success of *The Blue
Angel.* They continued to work
together occasionally, and

in 1939 he composed the
rousing numbers for her film
Destry Rides Again, including
'The Boys In The Back Room'.
Hollander scored dozens of
films in the USA, including
musicals for another exotic
chanteuse, Dorothy Lamour, as
well as one of the oddest
fantasies ever filmed: *The 5,000
Fingers Of Dr T,* with script and
lyrics by Dr Seuss.

*One of the many beautiful
studio portraits of
Marlene Dietrich taken
when she had established
herself in Hollywood.*

*Following pages
One of the most famous
film stills of all time…
Dietrich's film début in*
The Blue Angel.

Falling In Love Again

Music & Original Words by Friedrich Hollander
English Words by Samuel Lerner

More Than You Know

Words by William Rose & Edward Eliscu
Music by Vincent Youmans

1. Whe - ther you are here or yon - der, whe - ther you are false or true,
(Verse 2 see block lyric)
whe - ther you re - main or wan - der, I'm grow - ing fond - er of you.

More Than You Know
1930
The evocative lyrics are by Billy Rose and Edward Eliscu, and the music is by a fine composer whose name is little remembered today: Vincent Youmans. He was one of the great figures of musical comedy's heyday, much admired by the Gershwins and other fellow songwriters, but his career was cut tragically short by tuberculosis. Among his best remembered hit songs are 'Tea For Two', 'I Want To Be Happy', 'Time On My Hands' and 'Without A Song'. His last work was the score for the 1933 movie *Flying Down To Rio* which first teamed Fred Astaire and Ginger Rogers.

New York, 1928:
One of the many victims
of the Wall Street Crash.

Ev - en tho' your friends for - sake you, ev - en tho' you don't suc - ceed,
would - n't I be glad to take you, give you the break you need. More than you
know, more than you know "Man" o' my heart I love you so, late - ly I find you're on my
"Girl"
mind, more than you know._ Whe - ther you're right, whe - ther you're wrong, "Man" o' my
"Girl"
heart, I'll come a - long, you need me so, more than you'll ev - er know,_
_ Lov - ing you the way that I do, there's no - thing I can do a - bout it,_
lov - ing may be all you can give but ho - ney I can't live with - out it.
Oh how I'd cry, oh how I'd cry, if you got tired and said "Good - bye" more than I'd
show, more than you ev - er know._ More than you know._

Verse 2:
When my heart is fill'd with sadness
And the dreary hours won't go
Just a word would bring me gladness
Altho' it's madness, I know
You are all the world to me, dear
I can love no-one but you
Happy in your arms I'll be, dear
So you can see, it's true.

Nightcaps at The Ritz hotel in Paris, a hot evening during the 1931 heatwave.

Goodnight Sweetheart

1931

This delightful song was the signature tune of bandleader and songwriter Ray Noble (see 'The Very Thought Of You', page 78). It also became a regular feature for another bandleader – the singer and actor Rudy Vallee. His early trade mark was to sing through a megaphone, and he was the first vocalist to be called a 'crooner'. Vallee's gentle delivery was perfectly suited to the intimacy of radio, where he became a huge star. He also appeared in movies, notably *Vagabond Lover* (1929), *Palm Beach Story* (1942) and *How To Succeed In Business Without Really Trying* (1967).

Goodnight Sweetheart

Words & Music by Ray Noble, Jimmy Campbell & Reg Connelly

Verse 2:
Such happy hours were spent together dear
And we will weather dear, the sad ones too.
Just put your trust in me and you will find
The future silver lined with sunny days in plenty.

As Time Goes By

Words & Music by Herman Hupfeld

Dooley Wilson and Humphrey Bogart take some time off during the filming of Casablanca.

As Time Goes By *1932*
How does a song become a standard? In this case, by a very tortuous route. Herman Hupfeld's best-remembered song was actually written for a revue in 1931, where it failed to create much excitement. It subsequently turned up in the stage play which was later adapted for the screen as *Casablanca*. (The song was very nearly dropped from the movie, as executives from the film studio, Warner Brothers, wanted instead to use a number by one of their contract writers.)

However, thanks to a magnificent rendition by Dooley Wilson, and one of the best dramatic set-ups a song has ever enjoyed on the silver screen, the number – at last – achieved its much-deserved success.

Hupfeld's other songs include 'Let's Put Out The Lights And Go To Sleep', 'Sing Something Simple', and 'Are You Making Any Money?' from the bizarrely-titled film, *Moonlight And Pretzels*.

Hoagy Carmichael, seen here rehearsing with his band, was an important American composer, pianist, singer, and even actor, from the Twenties onwards.

Georgia On My Mind *1932*

The lyric writer for this great Hoagy Carmichael tune was Stuart Gorrell, a college friend of Hoagy's who never wrote another song (but who did suggest the title for one more Carmichael standard, 'Stardust'.) The smash-hit recording by Ray Charles in 1959 prompted the Georgia state legislature to make it the official state song.

Georgia On My Mind

Words by Stuart Gorrell
Music by Hoagy Carmichael

Underneath The Arches

Words & Music by Bud Flanagan

Underneath The Arches

1932

This charming and nostalgic number, in the tradition of the British music hall, was written by Bud Flanagan of the much-loved double act, Flanagan and Allen. They also formed part of The Crazy Gang with two other double acts – Nervo and Knox, and Naughton and Gold – plus the eccentric juggler and knockabout comedian "Monsewer" Eddie Gray.

One of the 'Hungerford Club', the homeless Londoners who congregated around the South Bank area of London near Hungerford Bridge that is now the Royal Festival Hall.

Try A Little Tenderness

Words & Music by Harry Woods, Jimmy Campbell & Reg Connelly

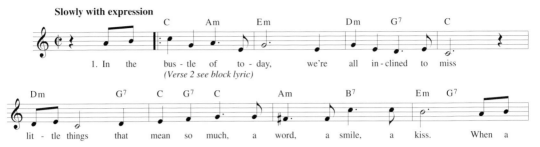

Slowly with expression

1. In the bus - tle of to - day, we're all in - clined to miss
(Verse 2 see block lyric)
lit - tle things that mean so much, a word, a smile, a kiss. When a

From Gold Digger's of 1933,
a typical scene created by
Busby Berkeley, the master of
the Thirties musicals.

Try A Little Tenderness
1933
The depression-era ditty 'Try A
Little Tenderness' dates originally
from the year 1933, when
bootleggers still plied their trade,
and other hits included 'Brother
Can You Spare A Dime'. It was
memorably revived by Otis
Redding in 1967 and then in
Alan Parker's hit film *The
Commitments*, proving that a great
standard can be rediscovered by
each new generation.

C / Am / Em / Dm / G7 / C
wo - man loves a man, he's a he - ro in her eyes, and a

D7 / G/B / E7 / A7 / Am7 / D7 / G / F / G
he - ro he can al - ways be, if he'll just re - a - lise.

C / Dm7 / G7 / C / Gm / A7
She may be wea - ry, wo - men do get wea - ry, wear - ing the same shab - by dress.

D7 / F / G9 / G7 / C/E / G7
And when she's wea - ry, try a lit - tle ten - der - ness.

C / Dm / G7 / C / Gm/B♭ / A7
You know she's wait - ing, just an - ti - ci - pat - ing, things she may ne - ver pos - sess.

D7 / F / G9 / G7 / C / C7
While she's with - out them, try a lit - tle ten - der - ness. It's

F / E7 / Am / C aug / A7
not just sen - ti - men - tal, she has her grief and care, and a

Dm / A7 / Dm / G9 / G7
word that's soft and gen - tle, makes it ea - si - er to bear.

C / Dm7 / G7 / C / Gm/B♭ / A7
You won't re - gret it, wo - men don't for - get it, love is their whole hap - pi - ness.

D7 / G9 / Dm7 / G7 / 1. C / F dim / C / 2. C
It's all so ea - sy, try a lit - tle ten - der - ness. 2. With a - ness.

Verse 2:
With a tender word of love
You can make the wrong things right.
Charm away the clouds of grey
And make this drab world bright.
When your worries drag you down
It's so easy to forget
But make the effort just the same
And see the thrill you'll get.

This song later provided the title for the movie by Peter Bogdanovich, Paper Moon, *set in the period and starring Ryan O'Neal and his young daughter Tatum, pictured below.*

It's Only A Paper Moon

1933

'It's Only A Paper Moon' was memorably introduced by Cliff "Ukelele Ike" Edwards, whose extraordinary career ranged from starring with Fred and Adele Astaire in the Gershwin musical *Lady Be Good* to playing the voice of Jiminy Cricket in Walt Disney's *Pinocchio*.

Music and lyrics by Harold Arlen and E.Y. "Yip" Harburg (see entry on 'Over The Rainbow' on page 98) with an assist from Billy Rose, prolific lyric writer, theatrical impresario and owner of leading New York night-spot, The Diamond Horseshoe.

Following pages Cab Calloway leads his orchestra at The Cotton Club in New York's Harlem in 1937

It's Only A Paper Moon

Music by Harold Arlen
Words by E.Y. Harburg & Billy Rose

Smoke Gets In Your Eyes

Music by Jerome Kern
Words by Otto Harbach

Slowly

They asked me how I knew my true love was true,

I of course re - plied, some - thing here in - side, can - not be de -

- nied. They said some - day you'll find all who love are

blind, when your heart's on fire, you must re - a -

- lize smoke gets in your eyes.

A little faster

So I chaffed them and I gay - ly laughed to think they could doubt my

love. Yet to - day my love has flown a - way. I am with - -

rit. *a tempo*

- out my love. Now laugh - ing friends de -

- ride, tears I can - not hide, so I smile and

say, "When a love - ly flame dies, smoke gets in your eyes."

Smoke Gets In Your Eyes
1933
Jerome Kern originally wrote the melody, inspired perhaps by Chopin's E Major Etude, as the signature tune for a radio series which never materialised. It was then used, again instrumentally, for a front-cloth tap routine to cover a scene change in *Show Boat*, but cut during an out-of-town try-out. And the twice-discarded tune might have languished forever in Kern's "trunk", had not lyricist Otto Harbach stumbled across the manuscript while working with Kern on the 1933 musical, *Roberta*.

"Why not change the tempo? It might make an attractive ballad," he suggested. Kern obliged, and the result was an instant hit in the Broadway stage show which sky-rocketed Bob Hope to fame. (The show was later filmed starring Irene Dunne and Fred Astaire.) The song was revived in 1959 by The Platters, who took it to number one in the US charts.

The cigarette was the essential fashion accessory. Here a pack of bathing beauties at Aldeburgh, Suffolk, enjoy a puff.

His master's voice? By the mid-Thirties the majority of British households had a wireless set.

The Very Thought Of You
1934

British pianist and band leader Ray Noble was also a gifted songwriter, and among his many other hits were 'Goodnight Sweetheart' (see page 62), 'Love Is The Sweetest Thing', 'The Touch Of Your Lips' and 'By The Fireside'. He was musical director for the HMV record label untill 1934, when he went to the US (with star vocalist Al Bowlly) to lead a band featuring Glenn Miller in New York's Rainbow Room. Noble found great success in the States, accompanying Fred Astaire on records, appearing as a dim Englishman on radio with George Burns and Gracie Allen, and guesting with his band in several films.

The Very Thought Of You

Words & Music by Ray Noble

Over My Shoulder

Words & Music by Harry Woods

Over My Shoulder *1934*

Hollywood had set the pace for musical movies with a cascade of *Gold Diggers* and *Big Broadcast* extravanganzas. And the British film studios – already well established for their outstanding dramatic pictures – responded with some delightful song-and-dance films. Many of them starred either the debonair Jack ('Everything Stops For Tea') Buchanan, or the elfin Jessie Matthews.

"She possessed freshness and natural high spirits in keeping with her tip-tilted nose, wide smile and china-blue, saucer eyes... she sang a clever little song with a complete semblance of spontaneity, and danced as one delighted to be dancing" – James Agate.

Jessie Matthews had already found huge success in the theatre, having risen from childhood poverty (dancing for pennies in the streets of Soho) to become one of the leading ladies of the West End stage. She became Britain's first musical superstar of the silver screen, acclaimed even in the USA. Her first starring film was *Evergreen*, which introduced this carefree, exuberant number – it instantly became her theme song – and began a dazzling series of musicals which included *First A Girl*, *It's Love Again*, and *Gangway*.

British musical movies had generally been screen versions of West End hits by Noel Gay, Ray Noble, Vivian Ellis and other "frightfully English" composers. However, for the Jessie Matthews films, top American songwriters were imported to add a little pizazz. Sigler, Goodhart & Hoffman were regular visitors to the British Gaumont studio, and Tin Pan Alley hit-maker Harry Woods (see 'Try A Little Tenderness') was called in to add new songs to the original stage score for *Evergreen* by Richard Rodgers and Lorenz Hart.

A dance hall in New York's Harlem in the early Thirties.

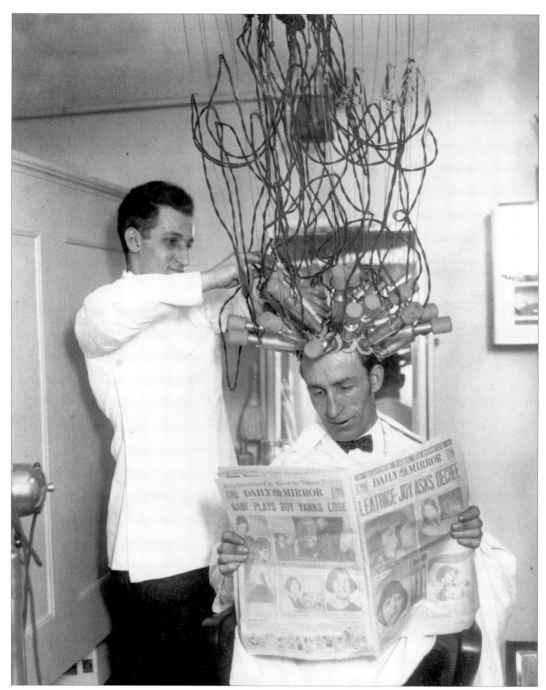

These Foolish Things *1936*
On the sheet music, the lyrics
are credited to "Holt Marvell",
a pen-name for the BBC radio
producer Eric Maschwitz, who
also liked to moonlight as a
lyricist and book-writer for the
musical theatre. (Other songs by
Maschwitz include 'Goodnight
Vienna' and 'A Nightingale
Sang In Berkeley Square'.) The
words were reputedly inspired
by his ex-wife, the vivacious and
eccentric actress Hermione
Gingold, and the song was
introduced by Cyril Ritchard
and Madge Elliott in the show
Spread It Abroad. Several artists
have made hit records of the
song, notably Frank Sinatra and
Billie Holiday.

New technology hits
the high street...
'Same perm as last
week, sir?'

These Foolish Things

Words by Eric Maschwitz
Music by Jack Strachey

Rather slowly

1. A ci-ga-rette that bears a lip-stick's tra-ces,—— an air-line tic-ket to ro-man-tic pla-ces.——

(Verses 2 & 3 see block lyric)

And still my heart has wings,—— these fool-ish things re-mind me of you.

A tink-ling pi-a-no in the next a-part-ment,—— those stumb-ling words that told you what my heart meant.——

A fair-ground's paint-ed swings,—— these fool-ish things re-mind me of you.

You came, you saw, you con-quer'd me. When you did that to me, I

some-how knew that this had to be. The winds of March that make my heart a dan-cer,——

a te-le-phone that rings but who's to an-swer?—— Oh how the ghost of you

clings! These fool-ish things—— re-mind me of you. you.

Verse 2:
Gardenia perfume lingering on a pillow
Wild strawberries only seven francs a kilo.
And still my heart has wings
These foolish things remind me of you.
The park at evening when the bell has sounded
The "Île de France" with all the gulls around it.
The beauty that is Spring's
These foolish things remind me of you.
I know that this was bound to be.
These things have haunted me
For you have entirely enchanted me.
The sigh of midnight trains in empty stations
Silk stockings thrown aside, dance invitations.
Oh how the ghost of you clings!
These foolish things remind me of you.

Verse 3:
First daffodils and long excited cables
And candlelight on little corner tables.
And still my heart has wings
These foolish things remind me of you.
The smile of Garbo and the scent of roses
The waiters whistling as the last bar closes.
The song that Crosby sings
These foolish things remind me of you.
How strange, how sweet, to find you still.
These things are dear to me
That seem to bring you so near to me.
The scent of smouldering leaves, the wail of steamers
Two lovers on the street who walk like dreamers.
Oh how the ghost of you clings!
These foolish things remind me of you.

The Way You Look Tonight

Music by Jerome Kern
Words by Dorothy Fields

Verse 2:
Oh, but you're lovely
With your smile so warm
And your cheek so soft.
There is nothing for me
But to love you
Just the way you look tonight.

The Way You Look Tonight
1936
This is among the very finest of songs from the magical series of Fred Astaire and Ginger Rogers musicals. Astaire danced divinely, of course, but he also sang superbly. The great songwriters loved to write for him, and they knew he would treat their songs with care, wit, intelligence, charm and

unerring musicianship. Writing for Astaire inevitably brought the very best out of such great talents as Irving Berlin, the Gershwins, Cole Porter, Vincent Youmans, Johnny Mercer, and Jerome Kern and Dorothy Fields with their shimmering score for *Swing Time*. It's packed with musical delights such as the sardonic love song 'A Fine Romance', which serves as a

perfect counterpoint to the Oscar-winning 'The Way You Look Tonight'.

Unusually, this song has a coda, "a series of precisely modulated hums that balance the stammers at the beginning" according to Robert Cushman, which is not usually performed, but can be heard on the 1942 recording by Peggy Lee with Benny Goodman.

Ginger Rogers and Fred Astaire in a scene from one of their later RKO musicals, Carefree from 1938.

Amy Johnson made a record solo flight from London to Cape Town and return in 1936. She drowned after bailing out over the Thames estuary.

Pennies From Heaven

1936

This Oscar-nominated movie title song was by two top-notch songwriters, Johnny Burke, whose many hits include 'Swinging On A Star' and 'Misty', and Arthur Johnston, writer of classics like 'Cocktails For Two', 'The Moon Got In My Eyes' and 'Thanks A Million'. Bing Crosby and Louis Armstrong co-starred in the movie (they were reunited twenty years later in *High Society*) and both had hits with the song. *Pennies From Heaven* was also the title of Dennis Potter's landmark British television drama about a sheet-music salesman, portrayed on BBC TV by Bob Hoskins, and then filmed for MGM in 1981 starring Steve Martin.

Pennies From Heaven

Words by John Burke
Music by Arthur Johnston

Summertime
(from *Porgy And Bess*)

Words & Music by George Gershwin, Ira Gershwin, DuBose & Dorothy Heyward

Summertime *1936*

George Gershwin composed an astonishing range of music, from Tin Pan Alley hits like 'Swanee' and theatre songs like 'Fascinating Rhythm' (both are in this book) to major concert works such as 'Rhapsody In Blue' and 'An American In Paris'. As his good friend Irving Berlin said "George Gershwin is the only songwriter I know who became a composer".

Gershwin's masterwork was *Porgy And Bess*, which he called a folk opera, because, as he wrote in the *New York Times*, "Porgy And Bess is a folk tale. Its people would naturally sing folk music. When I first began work on the music, I decided against the use of original folk material because I wanted the music to be all of one piece. Therefore I wrote my own spirituals and folksongs. But they are still folk music, and therefore, being in operatic form, *Porgy And Bess* becomes a folk opera."

'Summertime' in particular has the grandeur and simplicity of a traditional lullaby, although it also carries the unmistakable signature of Gershwin. The beautiful words are by the poet, author and folklorist DuBose Heyward, who wrote the original novel, the libretto and some of the lyrics.

Two years after his abdication and exiled in the south of France, ex-King Edward with his wife, the former Mrs Simpson. This was the first official photograph of them at their home, the Villa La Croe at Cap D'Antibes, Cannes.

Thanks For The Memory
1938
This wonderful number from the Paramount musical *Big Broadcast* of 1938 instantly became Bob Hope's theme song. Songwriters Ralph Rainger & Leo Robin were jointly responsible for dozens of hits, including 'Love In Bloom' which became the signature tune of another great comedian, Jack Benny. Leo Robin also wrote with other composers, and his lyrics range from 'Louise' for Maurice Chevalier in 1929 right through to *Gentlemen Prefer Blondes* with its enduring hit, 'Diamonds Are A Girl's Best Friend'.

Thanks For The Memory

Words by Leo Robin
Music by Ralph Rainger

Verse 2:

Thanks for the memory of sentimental verse, nothing in my purse
And chuckles when the preacher said "For better or for worse".
How lovely it was!
Thanks for the memory of lingerie with lace, Pilsner by the case
And how I jumped the day you trumped my one and only ace.
How lovely it was!

We said goodbye with a highball; and then I got "high as a steeple"
But we were intelligent people; no tears, no fuss
Hurray for us.
So thanks for the memory and strictly entre-nous, darling how are you?
And how are all the little dreams that never did come true?
Awfully glad I met you, cheerio and toodle-oo
And thank you so much!

Run, Rabbit, Run

Music by Noel Gay
Words by Noel Gay & Ralph Butler

Moderately

1. On the farm,— ev-'ry Fri - day, on the farm,—
(Verse 2 see block lyric)

— it's rab - bit pie— day. So ev - 'ry Fri - day, that

e - ver comes a - long, I get up ear - ly and sing this lit - tle song.

Run rab - bit, run rab - bit, run, run, run. Run rab - bit,

run rab - bit, run, run, run. Bang, bang, bang, bang,

goes the far - mer's gun. Run rab - bit, run rab - bit, run, run,

run. Run rab - bit, run rab - bit, run, run, run.

Don't give the far - mer his fun, fun, fun. He'll get

by with - out his rab - bit pie. So run rab - bit, run rab - bit,

1.
run, run, run.

2.
run, run, run.

Verse 2:
On the farm, no poor rabbit
Comes to harm because I grab it.
They jump and frolic
Whenever I go by.
They know I help 'em
To dodge the rabbit pie.

Run, Rabbit, Run
1939
During the war, a news item about bunnies being strafed in the Shetlands by the Luftwaffe gave this song (from a revue at the London Palladium called *The Little Dog Laughed*) an extra topical boost. The words and music were by Ralph Butler and Noel Gay.

In the run up to the Battle of Britain, RAF pilots practise a 'scramble' for the benefit of the news cameras at an air station somewhere in the south of England.

Following pages
July, 1941: Life goes on in the heavily bombed port of Plymouth… dancing on the sea front, complete with barrage balloon.

We'll Meet Again

Words & Music by Ross Parker & Hughie Charles

Moderately with expression

1. Let's say good-bye with a smile dear,—— just for a while dear,—— we must part.
(Verse 2 see block lyric)

Don't let the part-ing up - set you,—— I'll not for - get you sweet - heart.

We'll Meet Again *1939*
Songwriters Ross Parker & Hughie Charles swiftly followed up their first success 'There'll Always Be An England' with this splendid song. 'We'll Meet Again' became the first wartime hit for Vera Lynn, soon to be nominated The Forces' Sweetheart. With its message of good cheer and optimism, it perfectly encapsulates the spirit of the time, and remains one of the most evocative songs of the war years. Its use by Stanley Kubrick in his film *Dr Strangelove* was a master-stroke of irony.

The 'Forces Sweetheart' Vera Lynn serving mugs of tea to soldiers and sailors from the mobile canteen she presented to the forces in Trafalgar Square.

Verse 2:
After the rain comes the rainbow
You'll see the rain go, never fear.
We two can wait for tomorrow
Goodbye to sorrow my dear.

Over The Rainbow *1939*
This is the song which was famously deleted, not just once but three times, after previews of *The Wizard Of Oz* suggested that cuts were needed in the running time. (Okay, but lose something else, for goodness sake!) However, rescued from the cutting room floor by MGM's Arthur Freed, the number went on to win an Academy Award and its rightful place in the pantheon of all-time great songs.

Over The Rainbow

Words by E.Y. Harburg
Music by Harold Arlen

Kiss The Boys Goodbye

Music by Victor Schertzinger
Words by Frank Loesser

Kiss The Boys Goodbye
1941

The title song of her movie *Kiss The Boys Goodbye* was a hit for Mary Martin, who had blazed to stardom on Broadway singing Cole Porter's 'My Heart Belongs To Daddy' to a chorus of boy dancers which included the young Gene Kelly. Mary Martin starred in several more movies (notably with Bing Crosby) before returning to her first love, the stage, where she headlined two smash hits, *South Pacific* and *The Sound Of Music*. She was the definitive Peter Pan for generations of American children, after the Broadway production in which she co-starred with Cyril Ritchard was televised in 1954 and became an annual Christmas event.

Another enduring song hit from the same movie was 'Sand In My Shoes'. Both numbers had lyrics by Frank Loesser (see 'Baby It's Cold Outside') and music by Victor Schertzinger, who was both a gifted composer and film director. Among his credits as director were this film, *The Birth Of The Blues* and the first two 'Road' movies with Hope and Crosby. His hit songs include 'I Remember You', 'Dream Lover' and 'Tangerine'.

A troop train leaves for the south coast packed with British troops bound for France, hopefully to stop the German advance.

The Last Time I Saw Paris
1941

Lyricist Oscar Hammerstein II relates how this intensely-felt song came to be written: "The Germans had just taken Paris and I couldn't get my mind on anything else at all. I loved the city very much and I hated the idea of it falling. I thought of the enemy tramping through the streets and taking all the gaiety and beauty of the hearts of the people there... And this was kind of a lament. When I called Jerry (Jerome Kern) and asked him to write some music for it, he almost fell dead. In all the years we'd been working together, this was the first time I had completed a lyric that he would have to set to music.

He always wrote the melody and then I would fit the words to it."

The song was quickly interpolated in the MGM musical *Lady Be Good* and won the Academy Award for Best Song of 1941.

The Last Time I Saw Paris

Music by Jerome Kern
Words by Oscar Hammerstein II

Moderately

The last time I saw Pa - ris, her heart was warm and gay, I heard the laugh - ter of her heart in ev - ery street ca - fé. The last time I saw Pa - ris, her trees were dressed for spring, and lov - ers walked be - neath those trees, and birds found songs to sing. I dodged the same old ta - xi cabs that I had dodged for years, the cho - rus of their squeak - y horns was mu - sic to my ears. The last time I saw Pa - ris, her heart was warm and gay. No mat - ter how they change her, I'll re - mem - ber her that way.

1. that way. The

2. way.

The White Cliffs Of Dover

Words by Nat Burton
Music by Walter Kent

Verse 2:

I may not be near, but I have no fear
History will prove it too.
When the tale is told t'will be as of old
For truth will always win through.
But be I far or near, that slogan still I'll hear
"Thumbs up!"
For when the dawn comes up

May, 1941: Just twenty miles over the Channel from the white cliffs of Dover, a German soldier keeps watch on the English coastline.

The White Cliffs Of Dover
1941

When America entered the Second World War, it was the cue for Hollywood and Tin Pan Alley to go into overdrive. Patriotic movies and songs were the order of the day. And so a reassuring anthem about the symbolic white cliffs of Dover was prepared for the war effort, not in dear old Blighty, but by the American team of Walter Kent and Nat Burton. (Would a British lyricist have envisaged bluebirds off the coast of Dover?) It was recorded by several singers, including

Bebe Daniels, the American actress who, with her husband Ben Lyon, continued living and working in London throughout the war years.

Spike Milligan recalls being a soldier in Italy during the battle for Cassino: "I was trying to find our battery's network on the wireless when I stumbled across the Forces network, and heard Anne Shelton singing 'The White Cliffs Of Dover'... I burst into tears."

Born in 1903 in Tacoma, Washington, Bing Crosby epitomised the relaxed style of the crooners of the Thirties and Forties. His casual style belied his professional attitude and a keen commercial instinct.

I'll Be Seeing You *1944*
Originally written in 1938, this emotionally-charged song acquired an extra resonance during the Second World War. The words were by Irving Kahal, with music by Sammy Fain, whose other hits include

'That Old Feeling', 'Love Is A Many Splendoured Thing', 'Secret Love' (from *Calamity Jane*) and the songs for Disney's *Peter Pan* and *Alice In Wonderland*.

The song was a big hit in 1944 for the "Old Groaner" himself, Bing Crosby, and later became Liberace's signature tune.

I'll Be Seeing You

Words by Irving Kahal
Music by Sammy Fain

Ev'ry Time We Say Goodbye

Words & Music by Cole Porter

*The day after D-Day, 1944.
Hitler was convinced that the
Normandy landings were a
feint and the main assault
would come north of the Seine
river. By the end of June,
Eisenhower had 850,000 men
and 150,000 vehicles ashore.*

Ev'ry Time We Say
Goodbye *1944*

A late hit for the incomparable
Cole Porter, whose many other
all-time standards include
'You're The Top', 'Let's Do It',
'True Love', 'Anything Goes',
'Just One Of Those Things' and
'Night And Day' (which also
became the title of his inevitable
bio-pic in 1946). The song was
introduced in the 1944 stage
revue *Seven Lively Arts*, produced
by Billy Rose , but found its
most enduring success when
recorded twelve years later by
Ella Fitzgerald.

More recently, the song was a
chart hit for Simply Red.

Duke Ellington, one of the most respected figures in the history of jazz. Born in Washington DC, he played professionally from the age of 17. In 1943 he conducted the first of nine annual concerts at Carnegie Hall, New York City.

I'm Beginning To See The Light *1944*

This gorgeous tune was put together by two great bandleaders, Harry James and Duke Ellington, and a star alto sax player, Johnny Hodges. Lyricist Don George must have felt outnumbered, but he certainly delivered the goods – the song became a solid hit for both Ellington and James (and also for Ella Fitzgerald and The Ink Spots) and has remained a jazz standard ever since.

Following pages One of the many dancehalls which were packed nightly throughout Britain during the war.

I'm Beginning To See The Light

Words & Music by Harry James, Duke Ellington, Johnny Hodges & Don George

There I've Said It Again

Words & Music by Redd Evans & Dave Mann

There I've Said It Again

1945

This song by Redd Evans and Dave Mann became one of the biggest hit records of its day, selling over three and a half million records in 1945 for Vaughn Monroe and his Orchestra (his arranger was Ray Conniff). In the Sixties, it became a number one hit in the US all over again, this time for Bobby Vinton.

Less than a year after the last Germans had left Paris, in late 1945 Christian Dior created his full-flowered 'New Look', the complete opposite to the skimpy look of wartime. All over the world, fashion magazines went into rhapsodies.

You'll Never Walk Alone
1945

Composer Richard Rodgers had two extraordinary careers in popular song. With the witty, elegant lyricist Lorenz Hart, he wrote a succession of hit shows and movies, yielding standards like 'Blue Moon', 'My Heart Stood Still', 'This Can't Be Love' and 'My Funny Valentine'. Then, with veteran wordsmith Oscar Hammerstein, he created yet another astounding run of successful musicals, beginning with *Oklahoma* in 1943, continuing with *Carousel*, where this song originated, and including *South Pacific*, *The King And I* and *The Sound Of Music*.

Though Frank Sinatra and Judy Garland both scored contemporary hits with this song, it found a new and unexpected audience many years later. In 1963, it was the third release, and the third number one hit, for the Merseybeat group Gerry and the Pacemakers. A few weeks later, it was being sung at Liverpool's football ground. Soon it had become British football's unofficial theme song. It's a great anthem of hope and perseverance, and it sounds magnificent when roared out by a vast crowd of fans. But the supporters probably have no idea that it comes from a Broadway musical by Rodgers and Hammerstein.

Following the surrender of Japan, crowds celebrate V-Day in New York's Times Square.

You'll Never Walk Alone

Music by Richard Rodgers
Words by Oscar Hammerstein II

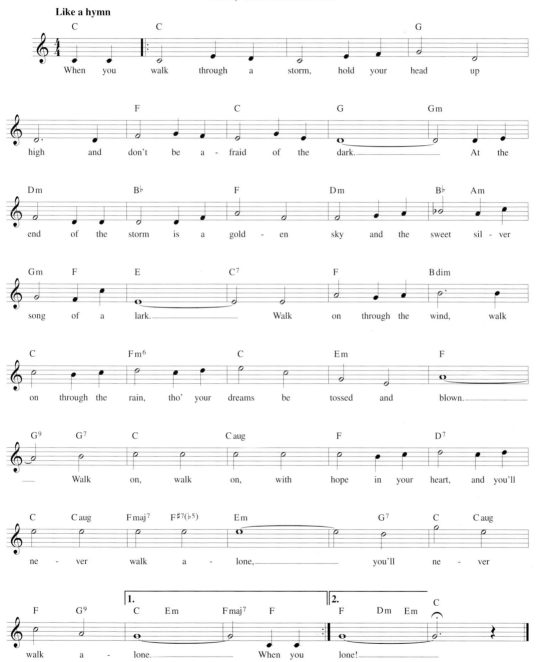

The Anniversary Song

Words & Music by Al Jolson & Saul Chaplin

1. Oh! how we danced on the night
(Verse 2 see block lyric)
we were wed, we vowed our true love
though a word was - n't said. The
world was in bloom, there we're stars in the
skies ex - cept for the few that were
there in your eyes. time.
Dear, as I held you so close in my arms, an - gels were
sing - ing a hymn to your charms, two hearts gent - ly beat - ing were
mur - mur - ing low "My dar - ling, I love you so." 2. The

Verse 2:
The night seemed to fade
Into blossoming dawn
The sun shone anew
But the dance lingered on
Could we but relive
That sweet moment sublime
We'd find that our love is unaltered by time.

May 8th, 1945: Winston Churchill speaks to the crowds, and to the nation on BBC radio, on VE Day in London's Whitehall .

The Anniversary Song
1946

The success of the bio-pic *The Jolson Story* – and the even greater success of its soundtrack album – gave Al Jolson the most remarkable comeback in popular music history. The self-styled "World's Greatest Entertainer" had been a huge draw in vaudeville, on Broadway, and in the early sound cinema. He was the star

of the first musical movie, *The Jazz Singer* in 1927, and spoke the now-famous line "You Ain't Heard Nothing Yet!" His signature songs included 'Swanee' , 'Toot Toot Tootsie' and 'My Mammy'. But in the Forties, with his melodramatic delivery and his continued use of "black-face", he was considered by producers to be hopelessly out-of-date – until *The Jolson Story* was released to enormous box-office success.

Among its five million-selling singles, 'The Anniversary Song'

proved the most enduring standard, though it was the only song actually written for the film (by Jolson himself with Saul Chaplin, based on a theme by Ivanovici). Saul Chaplin also composed hits like 'Shoeshine Boy' and 'Bei Mir Bist Du Schon', and later became an important arranger for movies ranging from *Kiss Me Kate* to *West Side Story*, for which he won an Oscar.

Carmen Miranda was one of the many stars of the late Forties who featured this great Peggy Lee song in her repertoire.

Mañana *1948*
This sunny samba was the USA top-selling new song of 1948, and took singer (and co-author) Peggy Lee soaring up the charts, eclipsing stars like Bing Crosby, Nat King Cole, Doris Day... even 'The Woody Woodpecker Song'.

Mañana (Is Good Enough For Me)

Words & Music by Peggy Lee & Dave Barbour

Samba

1. The fau - cet she is drip - ping and the fence she's fall - ing down. My
(Verses 2, 3, 4 & 5 see block lyric)
poc - ket needs some mon - ey, so I can't go in - to town. My
bro - ther is - n't work - ing and my sis - ter does - n't care. The
car, she needs a mo - tor, so I can't go a - ny - where. Ma -
- ña - na, ma - ña - na, ma - ña - na is
soon e - nough for me.　　2. My

Verse 2:
My mother's always working; she's working very hard.
But every time she looks for me, I'm sleeping in the yard.
My mother thinks I'm lazy and maybe she is right.
I'll go to work mañana, but I gotta sleep tonight.

Verse 3:
Oh, once I had some money, but I gave it to my friend.
He said he'd pay me double, it was only for a lend.
But he said a little later that the horse she was so slow.
Why he gave the horse my money is something I don't know.

Verse 4:
My brother took his suitcase and he went away to school.
My father said he only learn'd to be a silly fool.
My father said that I shoud learn to make a chilli pot.
But then I burn'd the house down, the chilli was too hot.

Verse 5:
The window she is broken and the rain is coming in.
If someone doesn't fix it, I'll be soaking to my skin.
But if we wait a day or two, the rain may go away.
And we don't need a window on such a sunny day.

Take Me To Your Heart Again
(La Vie En Rose)

Music by R.S. Louiguy
English Lyric by Frank Eyton

Steadily

Take me to your heart a-gain, let's make a start a-gain, for-giv-ing and for-get - - ting. Take me to your heart a-gain, and leave be-hind from then, a life of lone re-gret - - ting. Dear - est, let's turn back the years, let smiles come af-ter tears, like sun-shine af-ter rain. I'm yearn-ing for you by night and by day, pray-ing I'll soon hear you say-ing "I love you". Then we'll ne-ver part a-gain, if you will take me to your heart a-

1. -gain.

2. -gain.

Take Me To Your Heart Again (La Vie En Rose)

1948

Even a collection of British and American hit songs must include one of the great French chansons of the century, 'La Vie En Rose', which also became a standard worldwide. A number of French entertainers were popular internationally, from the legendary Mistinguett and Maurice Chevalier to singers such as Charles Trenet, with his hits 'Boum' and 'La Mer (Beyond The Sea)'. But perhaps the greatest impact was made by one of the most diminutive performers, the "little waif sparrow", Edith Piaf.

Following pages
November 1949: The 100
Club, Oxford Street, London.
Humphrey Lyttelton's band
plays New Orleans jazz.

Baby It's Cold Outside

Words & Music by Frank Loesser

Loesserando

1. I real - ly can't stay ___ I've got to go 'way, ___
(Verse 2 see block lyric)

1. But ba - by it's cold ___ out - side! But ba - by it's cold ___
(Verse 2 see block lyric)

this eve - ning has been ___ so ve - ry nice. ___

out - side! Been hop - ing that you'd drop in! I'll hold your hands

My moth - er will start to wor - ry ___ and fath - er will be pac - ing the

they're just like ice. Beau - ti - ful, what's your hur - ry?

floor, so real - ly I'd bet - ter scur - ry. ___ Well, may - be just a half a drink

Lis - ten to the fi - re - place roar! Beau - ti - ful, please, don't hur - ry ___

*January, 1947:
A snow-bound motorist
in Kent tries to navigate
a route through one of
the very worst British
winters on record.*

Baby It's Cold Outside
1949
This delicious duet between
The Wolf and The Mouse was
written as an amusement for
Frank Loesser's family and
friends. Luckily for posterity, he
was persuaded to include it in
the film *Neptune's Daughter* where
it was performed by MGM's
bathing beauty, Esther
"Dangerous When Wet"
Williams, and Ricardo
Montalban. It won the Oscar
for best motion picture song of
the year.
    Trivia note for sheet music
buffs: Many of his songs are
marked Tempo Moderato, but
this one bears the simple
instruction "Loesserando".

Voice 1, verse 2:
I simply must go
The answer is no!
The welcome has been so nice and warm
My sister will be suspicious
My brother will be there at the door
My maiden aunt's mind is vicious
Well, maybe just a cigarette more
I've got to get home
Say, lend me a comb
You've really been grand but don't you see
There's bound to be talk tomorrow
At least there will be plenty implied
I really can't stay
Ah, but it's cold outside.

Voice 2, verse 2:
But baby it's cold outside!
But baby it's cold outside!
How lucky that you dropped in!
Look out the window at that storm
Gosh, your lips look delicious
Waves upon a tropical shore!
Gosh, your lips are delicious
Never such a blizzard before
But, baby, you'd freeze out there
It's up to your knees out there
I thrill when you touch my hand
How can you do this thing to me
Think of my life-long sorrow
If you caught pnuemonia and died
Get over that old doubt
Baby, it's cold outside.

Unchained Melody

The Righteous Brothers
1965 – UK: 14, US: 4;
1990 – UK: 1

In the conservative pop scene of the early Fifties, ballads were often the order of the day (Frankie Laine had spent 18 weeks at number one with 'I Believe' in 1951). 'Unchained Melody' is one of those archetypal songs that reaches across so many boundaries it will probably be a hit every time a new generation hear it. In 1955 no less than three singers had a hit with it: Jimmy Young, Al Hibbler, and Les Baxter.

The US had another two versions by Roy Hamilton (US: 6) and June Valli (29). The song was featured in the film *Unchained*. In the last week of May all three were in the Top 10 at the same time. Hibbler won, taking the record to number one in the UK for three weeks in June-July but even then Young managed a number two when Hibbler's version fell to three. The version by The Righteous Brothers (Bill Medley and Bobby Hatfield), famous for 'You've Lost That Loving Feeling', was produced by Phil

'Wall Of Sound' Spector in 1965. In 1990 the same record was the top single of the year.

'Unchained Melody' is a powerfully uncluttered song, starting with the famous Fifties 'doo-wop' sequence and expressing a strong, focused emotion. It describes a world of wholly unambiguous feeling. Unlike life, here there are no ifs or buts, and music itself becomes the metaphor for the unleashed emotions.

Before its re-release hit in the Sixties, 'Unchained Melody' was a favourite at Fifties student parties.

Unchained Melody

Words by Hy Zaret
Music by Alex North

Moderately slow

Oh my love, my dar-ling, I've hun-gered for your touch a

long, lone-ly time. Time goes by so slow-ly, and

time can do so much. Are you still mine? I need your love,

I need your love, God speed your love to me. *Fine*

1. Lone-ly ri-vers flow to the sea, to the sea,
(Verse 2 see block lyric)

to the o-pen arms of the sea.

Lone-ly ri-vers sigh, wait for me, wait for me,

I'll be com-ing home, wait for me! -way. *D.C. al Fine*

Verse 2:
Lonely mountains gaze at the stars
At the stars
Waiting for the dawn of the day.
All alone I gaze at the stars
At the stars
Dreaming of my love far away.

Rock Around The Clock

Words & Music by Max C. Freedman & Jimmy de Knight

Swing Shuffle

One, two, three o'-clock, four o'-clock rock. Five, six, se-ven o'-clock, eight o'-clock rock.

Nine, ten, e-le-ven o'-clock, twelve o'-clock rock. We're gon-na rock a-round the

clock to-night.— 1. Put your glad rags on and join me hon',— we'll have some fun when the
(Verses 2, 3, 4 & 5 see block lyric)

clock strikes one.— We're gon-na rock a-round the clock to-night,— we're gon-na

rock, rock, rock till broad day-light.— We're gon-na rock, gon-na rock a-round

1-4. the clock— to-night.— 2. When the **5.**

Verse 2:
When the clock strikes two and three and four
If the band slows down we'll yell for more.
We're gonna rock around the clock tonight
We're gonna rock, rock, rock till broad daylight
We're gonna rock, gonna rock around the clock tonight.

Verse 3:
When the chimes ring five and six and seven
We'll be rockin' up in seventh heaven.
We're gonna rock around the clock tonight
We're gonna rock, rock, rock till broad daylight
We're gonna rock, gonna rock around the clock tonight.

Verse 4:
When it's eight, nine, ten, eleven, too
I'll be goin' strong and so will you.
We're gonna rock around the clock tonight
We're gonna rock, rock, rock till broad daylight
We're gonna rock, gonna rock around the clock tonight.

Verse 5:
When the clock strikes twelve, we'll cool off then
Start a rockin' 'round the clock again.
We're gonna rock around the clock tonight
We're gonna rock, rock, rock till broad daylight
We're gonna rock, gonna rock around the clock tonight.

A barrier stops the audience swarming over their idols at a rock'n'roll concert at Loew's State Theatre, Times Square, early in 1959.

Rock Around The Clock

Bill Haley & The Comets
1955 – UK: 1; US: 1

Arguments about which was the first true rock'n'roll record will go on forever, but this was the one that told the world rock'n'roll was here. Thirty-year-old Bill Haley and his Comets must have been as surprised as anyone when 'Rock Around The Clock', a song from the teen film *Blackboard Jungle*, became a worldwide number one on its re-release.

The swing feel and the prominent brass show the dying influence of the big-band sound. It's a simple 12-bar with one of the earliest rock guitar solos, full of tripping rhythms and classic Fifties semi-tone bends. Back then, if you could play Danny Cedrone's lead break you were one swinging hep-cat.

The lyric appeal of 'Rock Around The Clock' was party time. It used the simple but effective device of cueing the verses by numbers (Chuck Berry did something similar in 'Reelin' And Rockin''). Haley went on to have several more hits, including 'See You Later Alligator' and 'Razzle Dazzle', which were essentially variations on the formula. By the Sixties the genial Haley was resigned to a life as a golden oldie, but the passing years and receding kiss curl never diminished the commitment with which, as he clutched a big semi-acoustic guitar to his barrel-like figure, he belted out 'Rock Around The Clock'.

Elvis Aaron Presley in the recording studio during the late Fifties.

Heartbreak Hotel

Elvis Presley
1956 – UK: 3; US: 1

'Heartbreak Hotel' charted for four months in 1956 in the UK and then again in the summer of 1971. It spent 22 weeks on the *Billboard* chart, eight at number one.

This is one helluva creepy record. 'Heartbreak Hotel' stands out in Elvis Presley's early catalogue because none of the other hits quite prepare us for it.

Some songs are all about atmosphere and the atmosphere is more than the sum of their parts. This is one such track,

a superb exercise in minimalism. Somehow the rampant energy of the young Presley is temporarily smothered. It flickers only in the smouldering extra syllables he attaches to the words at the end of each verse as he edges his way into the chorus. For much of 'Heartbreak Hotel' Elvis is left almost on his own, his voice echoing in the Sun Studio reverb while the band punctuate the gloom with the odd chord. The lyric is full of shady lost souls like the bell-hop, turning an urban building into something out of Dante's purgatory.

Heartbreak Hotel

Words & Music by Mae Boren Axton, Tommy Durden & Elvis Presley

Blues Tempo

1. Now since my ba-by left me, I've found a new place to dwell, down at the end of lone-ly street at Heart-break Ho-tel. I'm so lone-ly, I'm so lone-ly, I'm so lone-ly that I could die. 2. And tho' it's al-ways crowd-ed, you can still find some room for bro-ken heart-ed lo-vers to cry there in the gloom and be so lone-ly, oh so lone-ly, oh so lone-ly they could die. 3. The bell-hop's tears keep flow-ing, the desk clerk's dressed in black.

(Verse 4 see block lyric)

They've been so long on lone-ly street, they ne-ver will go back. And they're so lone-ly, oh they're so lone-ly, they're so lone-ly they pray to die. 4. So die.

1. C
2. C6

Verse 4:
So if your baby leaves and you have a tale to tell
Just take a walk down lonely street to Heartbreak Hotel
Where you'll be lonely and I'll be lonely
We'll be so lonely that we could die.

Blue Suede Shoes

Words & Music by Carl Lee Perkins

Verse 3:
Burn my house, steal my car
Drink my liquor from my old fruit jar
Do anything that you want to do
But uh-uh honey lay off of my shoes.
Don't you step on my blue suede shoes.
You can do anything
But lay off of my blue suede shoes.

Blue Suede Shoes

Elvis Presley
1956 – UK: 9; US: 20)

In the summer of 1956 Elvis and Carl Perkins both took 'Blue Suede Shoes' into the UK Top Twenty and in the US Perkins' slower version was the bigger hit. However, the song has always been remembered as Elvis'. John Lennon once remarked of popular music that before Elvis there was nothing. As this book demonstrates, that isn't quite true, but Lennon put his finger on the seismic shift in the mid-Fifties when the rebellious, highly sexual energy of

rock'n'roll exploded as the soundtrack to the birth of the teenager. Rock'n'roll was an amalgam of white and black musical styles and as such its very existence threatened the segregationism of the American South. It was bought by newly moneyed teenagers and performed by musicians who were roughly the same age. At the centre was the figure of the moody rebel and among the musicians it was Elvis who personified this better than anyone.

With 'Blue Suede Shoes' Elvis gave rock'n'roll one of its most

enduring images. Musically it's a simple 12-bar with stabbing chords punctuating the verse, a snapping snare driving it throughout and Scotty Moore's elegant but energetic rhythm guitar. RCA tried to copy this sound once they'd signed Elvis but later tracks like 'Hard Headed Woman' or 'Big Hunk O'Love' have a forced, stagey quality compared to the youthful joy of Elvis' earliest tracks. Was there ever a talent that burned so brightly and diminished so quickly?

The 2Is coffee bar in Old Compton Street, in London's Soho. The birthplace of British rock'n'roll, it spawned stars such as Cliff Richard, Tommy Steele and Joe Brown.

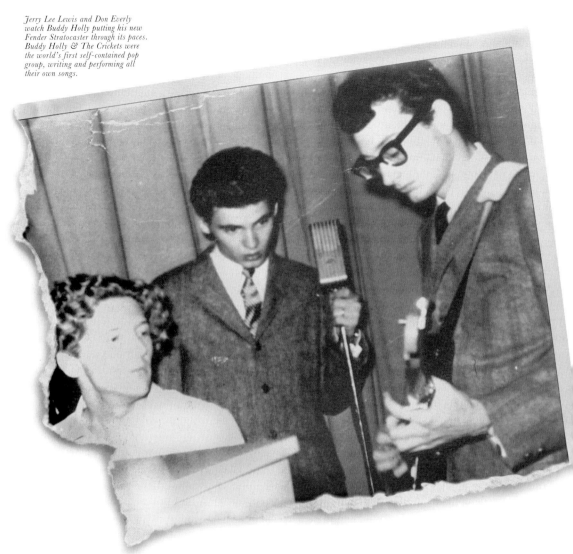

That'll Be The Day

Buddy Holly & The Crickets
1957 – UK: 1; US: 1

Bespectacled Buddy Holly made an unlikely rock'n'roller. He was a gawky 21-year-old from Texas with a strange hiccup in his voice and a neat suit, madly strumming a gizmo that looked like it came from Mars but was actually crafted by one Leo Fender, who named his new guitar the Stratocaster. The Crickets – Niki Sullivan, Jerry Allison and Joel B. Maudlin – fleshed out Holly's three-chord wonders. In this era most performers depended on

material written by songwriters, but with songs like 'Maybe Baby', 'Peggy Sue', 'Everyday', and 'Rave On', Holly showed you could write your own hits.

Whatever Holly sang had a certain optimism. 'That'll Be The Day' has it, capturing that significant moment when a young man realises that maybe he does have the strength to walk away and call her bluff.

Or is it that simple? Does the hook spring from confidence or bluster? Which ever way, a million listeners felt they understood. Holly's career came to a tragic end on February 3, 1959, when a crazily-organised winter tour and human error led to his death in a plane crash, along with Ritchie Valens and the Big Bopper. The event was immortalised in song by Don McLean in 'American Pie'. Meanwhile, back in England a bunch of Liverpool kids thrilled by Holly's example worked hard on their guitar-playing and perfecting that hiccup.

That'll Be The Day

Words & Music by Norman Petty, Buddy Holly & Jerry Allison

Summertime Blues

Words & Music by Eddie Cochran & Jerry Capehart

Verse 3:

I'm gonna take two weeks
Gonna have a fine vacation
I'm gonna take my problem
To the United Nations!

Well I called my Congressman
And he said (quote)
"Now I'd like to help you son,
But you're too young to vote."

Summertime Blues

Eddie Cochran
1958 – US: 8

Cochran's death in a car crash in April 1960 when he was 21 seemed to halt the march of rock'n'roll. In two successful years he released a brace of singles, one album, and appeared in films like *The Girl Can't Help It* and *Untamed Youth*.

His output shows a genuine talent that could reproduce most styles of late Fifties pop and R&B. 'Twenty Flight Rock' showed Cochran emulating Berry's self-deprecating humour and tracks like 'Eddie's Blues' and 'Sittin' In The Balcony' show his playing was up with the best rock guitarists of the time. Cochran was also an early pioneer of production techniques and overdubs.

Above all, Cochran gave us 'C'mon Everybody', 'Somethin' Else' (covered by The Sex Pistols) and 'Summertime Blues' (covered by The Who). What the Pistols didn't owe to Berry they owed to Cochran, and their Nineties heirs, like Green Day, carry that semitone bass figure on.

Even after 40 years the battering snare-drum on 'Somethin' Else' is still astonishing. 'Summertime Blues' is a classic expression of teen frustration, where nothing seems to work out with Authority – your parents, your boss or your congressman. Their opposition is in the voice-over that interrupts each verse. This break, coupled with a second to let Cochran sing the hook, helped to make the song unforgettable.

East Side Story: New York teenagers gather in the late Fifties on an avenue in New York's lower East Side.

This photograph of Chuck Berry doing h[is] famous 'duck walk' became an icon of Fifties rock'n'roll.

Johnny B Goode
Chuck Berry
1958 – US: 8

Along with Elvis, Chuck Berry was the great populariser of rock'n'roll in the Fifties, with his boogie 12-bars and patented guitar licks. Berry's songs voiced the concerns of the emerging teenager, capturing forever an idealised America of jukeboxes, soda fountains, and hot cars, the male in pursuit of the bobby-soxed female. His words are often witty – as in the case of 'Little Queenie', 'Roll Over Beethoven' and 'No Particular Place To Go', where he can't

get her seatbelt undone, and 'Sweet Little Sixteen' name-checked half the USA's geography. Like most of Berry's songs, 'Johnny B. Goode' is easy to play and has long since become a staple of pub and club bands everywhere.

It's a narrative lyric, the story of a boy from a poor log cabin in Lousiana who finds stardom. It sums up the dream of every struggling musician, black or white, and by extension the rags-to-riches myth of the American Dream itself. Johnny is Everyman, risen from

nothing; he just happens to be a guitar-player. We all want him to succeed, so Berry's refrain 'Go Johnny Go!' is ours too. The song also did much to mythologise the rock guitarist. Without Berry it's hard to imagine The Beatles or The Stones. Of the trillion or so covers the one you really need to hear is Hendrix's high-octane loose jam recorded at Berkeley in 1970, where the guitar man of his era thanks Chuck for writing his intro before blazing his way to glory.

Johnny B Goode

Words & Music by Chuck Berry

Verse 2:
He used to carry his guitar in a gunny sack
Go sit beneath the tree by the railroad track.
Ol' engineer in the train sittin' in the shade
Strummin' with the rhythm that the drivers made.
The people passin' by, they would stop and stare
Oh my, but that little country boy could play.

Verse 3:
His mother told him, "Someday you will be a man
And you will be the leader of a big old band.
Many people comin' from miles around
To hear you play your music till the sun goes down.
Maybe some day your name'll be in lights
A-sayin' Johnny B. Goode tonight."

All I Have To Do Is Dream

Words & Music by Boudleaux Bryant

Verse 2:
When I feel blue in the night
And I need you to hold me tight.
Whenever I want you all I have to do is
Dream, dream, dream, dream.

As well as American music, the post-war British teenagers embraced everything from the USA, from Coca-Cola to Cadilacs.

All I Have To Do Is Dream

The Everly Brothers
1958 - UK: 1; US: 1

Few male duets have been as successful or as influential as The Everly Brothers. Signed in 1956, Phil and Don Everly established an unmistakable vocal style with 'Bye Bye Love' in 1957. Over country-rock backings and prominent acoustic guitar, the Everlys sang melodies in almost unbroken two-part harmony, their voices blending uncannily. Many Everly hits were written by the husband and wife team of Boudleaux and Felice Bryant, though 'Till I Kissed You' came from Don Everly himself. The Everlys' presence loomed large in popular music in that strange lull between the death of Buddy Holly and 'Love Me Do'. They recorded impeccable ballads like 'Let It Be Me' and carried the country-rock torch on tracks like 'Rip It Up' and Orbison's choppy 'Claudette'. It's easy to imagine Eddie Cochran singing 'Wake Up Little Susie', a song whose lyrics were once considered too suggestive!

In contrast to the fierce strumming of their uptempo tunes, 'All I Have To Do Is Dream' is gentleness personified, drifting from the opening hook of 'dream, dream, dream' through its doo-wop sequence (I-VI-IV-V with variation of I-VI-II-V) to its bridge and back again. From the shivering tremolo electric guitar to the light percussion, nothing is allowed to obstruct the vocal harmony sustained throughout.

Glenn Campbell and Bobbie Gentry took this to number three in the UK and 27 in the US in 1970.

Although at first he rejected running for the presidency, Dwight Eisenhower yielded to the liberal Republicans in 1952. As a war hero of enormous popularity, he appealed to many Democrats as well. When he ran again in 1956, the first election to really benefit from advertising and TV, his majority was 9.5 million.

Cathy's Clown

Everly Brothers
1960 – UK: 1; US: 1

Did a vocal harmony ever cast its spell so quickly and so devastatingly as the opening of 'Cathy's Clown'? As the Everlys' sing 'love', the lower note holds as the higher spirals down toward it, through shades of hurt with each interval formed and dissolved. Underneath, a tight, almost martial snare-drum with whipped guitar chords drills the simplest of chord changes, as if for a public execution by shame. When the boys swoon on the D minor – 'I die each time' – it's as if the emotion has become too much, but somehow they pull themselves up for the B flat major under 'I hear this sound' before repeating that marvellous hook.

'Cathy's Clown' was the UK's best-selling single in 1960, the year the Everlys made history by signing the first million-dollar contract with Warner Bros. Changes in pop music soon left them high and dry, but this is arguably their finest moment, to which The Beatles' paid homage with the harmony on 'Please Please Me'.

Cathy's Clown

Words & Music by Don Everly

Moderately

1. I've got to stand tall,_____ you know a man__ can't crawl.

(Verse 2 see block lyric)

For when he knows you tell lies and he lets them pass by, then he's not a man at all._____

_____ Don't want your love_____ a - ny - more, don't want your

kiss - - - es that's for sure. I die each time_____

_____ I hear this sound. Here he comes,_____ that's Ca - thy's

1. clown._____ 2. When you see me shed a

2. clown._____

Verse 2:
When you see me shed a tear
And you know that it's sincere
Don't you think it's kind of sad
That you're treating me so bad
Or don't you even care?

Save The Last Dance For Me

Words & Music by Doc Pomus & Mort Shuman

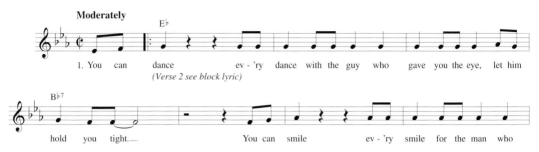

Moderately

1. You can dance ev-'ry dance with the guy who gave you the eye, let him
(Verse 2 see block lyric)

hold you tight.___ You can smile ev-'ry smile for the man who

Save The Last Dance For Me

The Drifters
1960 – UK: 2; US: 1

After a re-launched Drifters appeared in 1959, hits came with 'There Goes My Baby' and continued through to 1964, with 'Up On The Roof', 'On Broadway', and 'Under The Boardwalk'. The Drifters were part of a Fifties group-vocal tradition that included outfits like The Coasters, The Platters and The Moonglows.

'Save The Last Dance For Me' became their biggest hit.

Ben E King is way out front of the other voices, bass, strummed guitar and slightly Spanish rhythm. Three major chords carry the tune; no minors are permitted to make the anxiety overt. The striking part is the lyric, for this is adult stuff. Few lyrics in pop have been this generous in their countenancing of a partner dancing with other suitors. 'Go and have your fun' sings King, and only the strangely elongated phrases hint how much this generosity costs the singer (that and the tight-lipped

'mmmms' at the end). By the last verse he is even talking about someone holding her tight in the pale moonlight... just as long as he has the last dance, and she goes home with him. We want to believe that such selflessness has a just and loving reward. Presumably that's what millions bought it for. Maybe they also sensed it was genuine: Doc Pomus, co-writer, often watched his wife dancing with other men from his wheelchair. Remember that next time someone tells you pop is fantasy.

The sexes divide at an early Sixties American High School dance.

Following pages July, 1958: Yet untouched by the rock'n'roll revolution...well behaved and smartly dressed young people enjoy an evening dance in Poe Park, the Bronx, New York City.

held your hand___ 'neath the pale moon-light.___ But don't for-get who's tak-ing you
home and in whose arms you're gon-na be.___ So dar-lin'___ save the

1.
last dance for me. 2. Oh I me.

Ba-by, don't you know I love you so?___ Can't you feel it when we touch?

I will ne-ver, ne-ver let you go,___ I love you oh so much.

You can dance, go and car-ry on___ till the night is gone,___ and it's

time to go.___ If he asks if you're all a-lone,___ can he

take you home,___ you must tell him no.___ 'Cause don't for-get who's tak-ing you

home and in whose arms you're gon-na be.___ So dar-lin'___ save the

1.
last dance for me.

2.
You can me.___

Verse 2:
Oh I know that the music is fine
Like sparkling wine
Go and have your fun.
Laugh and sing
But while we're apart
Don't give your heart to anyone.

Leather-clad 'ton-up' bikers gather around the jukebox at a transport cafe on London's North Circular Road.

Only The Lonely

Roy Orbison
1960 – UK: 1; US: 2

Born in Texas in 1936, Orbison started as a rockabilly singer, working at Sun Records in the magic year of 1956. 'Only The Lonely' was Orbison's third single for RCA, and went massive just about everywhere. It ushered in four years of hits that included 'It's Over', 'Pretty Woman', 'Crying', 'In Dreams', and 'Running Scared'. People forget how successful he was in the early Sixties, racking up 16 Top Twenty hits in the UK. Onstage he didn't gyrate like Elvis, he just stood there, the Man in Black with his trade mark dark glasses. It was the power of his voice that delivered.

Some of Orbison's hits can sound overblown to modern ears. But early in the Sixties they aspired to a grandeur few records could match. Many are like mini-operas, chunks of reverb-laden drama that heave their way to a climax in two-and-half minutes before crashing into silence. 'Only The Lonely' is a gentler, shuffling discourse on loneliness with catchy backing vocals ('oh yeah-yeah-yeah'), high piano, and an active bass. The characteristic Orbison melodrama is restrained on this, felt only with the orchestra and female voices behind the phrases 'there goes my baby' and 'maybe tomorrow'. It's a very fluid song too: verse and chorus melt into one another, the hook coming back faster than you expect before Orbison wraps it all up with a brief falsetto flourish.

Only The Lonely

Words & Music by Roy Orbison & Joe Melson

Verse 2:
Only the lonely know the heartaches I've been through
Only the lonely know I cry and cry for you
Maybe tomorrow, a new romance
No more sorrow, but that's the chance
You've got to take if you're lonely
Heartbreak, only the lonely

Moon River

Words by Johnny Mercer
Music by Henry Mancini

Moon River

1961-
*UK: 1 [Danny Willaims]; US: 11
(Jerry Butler) & 11 (Henry
Mancini)*
Jerry Butler and Henry Mancini
took versions of 'Moon River'
into the US charts and in the
UK it was covered successfully
by Danny Williams. The song
was featured in the film *Breakfast
At Tiffany's* and is possibly one of
the last examples of a song that
charted in several versions at
once, a phenomenon common
in the Fifties that became rarer
as the Sixties progressed.

The lyric appears to be about
exploring the world, hence the
allusion to *Huckleberry Finn* and
the imagery of two drifters off to
see the world – 'There's such a
lot of world to see'. However,
when heard out of context of
the film, the night-time image of
the title, references to the
rainbow's end and the
'heartbreaker' all suggest
something darker, a fatalism
which the music does nothing to
dispel.

The melody opens with an
expressive leap and maintains a
premium quality throughout as
it negotiates eddying chord
changes over an undulating
waltz rhythm. By the end,
curiosity about the world has
been eclipsed by a death-wish.
The 'Moon River' which is
'wider than a mile' leaves us
thinking not so much of earthly
exploration as the river that
runs round Hades. As Irish poet
W.B.Yeats wrote, 'What
disturbs our blood / Is but its
longing for the tomb'.

Audrey Hepburn takes her
Breakfast At Tiffany's.
A still from the 1961
Blake Edwards film of
Truman Capote's novella.

July 10, 1962: The world's first TV satellite flashed a picture to British TV screens for two minutes. An official diagram showing the satellite and its tracking stations.

ANDOVER, MAINE

HOLMDEL, N. J.

Telstar
The Tornados
1962 – UK: 1; US: 1

Joe Meek, the writer and producer of 'Telstar' was more than simply Britain's first real independent producer. He was a pioneer in the art of record production who threw away the rule book, a neurotic genius forever tinkling with his home-made machines in order to press forward the boundaries of recorded sound. He worked for various record companies and was usually fired for doing things he shouldn't, and in the end he wound up with his own make-shift studio above a shop in north London. It is therefore all the more remarkable that the second ever UK record to reach number one in the US (the first was also an instrumental – Acker Bilk's 'Stranger On The Shore', also 1962) should have been recorded not in a professional studio but in someone's attic.

Named after an early communications satellite, 'Telstar' was the first successful incorporation of synthesized sound into a pop hit; the catchy but simple melody performed on an early electronic organ, the whole piece enhanced by a triumphant upward key change before the final verse. Its powerful sound effects remain striking to this day and are a credit to Meek's genius for futuristic ideas. Unfortunately Meek found himself unable to compete with the post-Beatle rush of British groups. Losing his key songwriter Geoff Goddard, the temperamental, homosexual Meek was beset with financial problems and he drifted into severe depression during the last two years of his life. In 1967, he committed suicide, shooting himself with a shotgun immediately after shooting his landlady who also died.

'Telstar' won an Ivor Novello Award in 1962, and is reputed to be former British Prime Minister Margaret Thatcher's favourite song. The Tornados enjoyed one more hit with 'Globetrotter' but faded from the scene after 1963.

Telstar

By Joe Meek

Blowin' In The Wind

Words & Music by Bob Dylan

Brightly

1. How ma - ny roads must — a man walk —— down be -
(Verses 2 & 3 see block lyric)
- fore you call him — a man? —— Yes — 'n'
how ma - ny seas must — a white dove —— sail be -
- fore she sleeps in —— the sand? —— Yes — 'n'
how ma - ny times must — the can - non balls —— fly be -
- fore they're —— for - ev - er banned? —— The
an - swer my friend is blow - in' in —— the wind, the

1, 2.
an - swer —— is blow - in' in —— the wind.

3. *rit.*
wind. —— The an - swer — is blow - in' in —— the wind.

Verse 2:
How many times must a man look up
Before he can see the sky?
Yes 'n' how many ears must one man have
Before he can hear people cry?
Yes 'n' how many deaths will it take till he knows
That too many people have died?

Verse 3:
How many years can a mountain exist
Before it's washed to the sea?
Yes 'n' how many years can some people exist
Before they're allowed to be free?
Yes 'n' how many times can a man turn his head
Pretending he just doesn't see?

Blowin' In The Wind

Bob Dylan
1962 – UK: 13; US: 2

Dylan arrived in the early Sixties as the heir apparent to Woody Guthrie's vacant throne. Armed only with an acoustic guitar and a harmonica, Dylan revolutionised the idea of what a pop lyric could express. Music *per se* was never the core of Dylan's art, as his indifference to arrangements and record production showed. His sneering, pitch-indifferent singing was itself a rejection of the Establishment, and gave his words a razor-sharp edge. His beat-poet lyrics became mazes of symbolism and twisted wordplay that challenged the listener. To move centre-stage all he needed was a backbeat. To howls of protest from some of his folk audience, Dylan went electric with his fifth album, *Bringing It All Back Home*, which secured his position as number one spokesman for American youth.

'Blowin' In The Wind' (*The Freewheelin' Bob Dylan*, 1962) is, along with 'I Shall Be Released', probably the most famous protest song of the period. The song is easy to play and for Dylan the lyric is actually straight-forward, organised around nine metaphorical questions, answered by the refrain. At the time it was read as anti-war, pro-civil rights. Unlike many of Dylan's songs, others could cover 'Blowin' In The Wind' and not look foolish. The song has been recorded many times, usually with additional sugar, with hit versions from Peter, Paul and Mary (1963) and Stevie Wonder (1968), and may have given Donovan the idea for a career.

July 1962: A ticker-tape welcome for President Kennedy and the First Lady on their trip to Mexico. The New York Times described it as giant fiesta rather than a state visit.

April 1963: John, George, Paul and Ringo film a TV studio scene at the Scala Cinema in London for their first feature film A Hard Day's Night.

She Loves You
The Beatles
1963 – UK: 1; US: 1
Yeah, yeah, yeah! This is the moment, dear reader, to point out that this book has a companion volume. It's called *The Beatles Complete*. Let's face it, for any selection of songs from the century to do justice to the Fab Four would mean no-one else got a look-in. Every period of The Beatles is chockfull of amazing songs – great tunes, great words, great recordings. In the grip of prog-rock's browbeating sense of self-importance Seventies' rock criticism dismissed songs like 'She Loves You', 'Please Please Me' and 'I Wanna Hold Your Hand'. If a song was shorter than three minutes and didn't have at least three time signatures and a long guitar solo, it must be fluff. But we have awoken from our sleep. 'She Loves You' is The Beatles in full mop-top glory with nifty chord changes, a subdominant minor ('love like that') to twang

the heartstrings, a few squirts of Chuck Berry lead to remind you of the Hamburg days, Ringo's brilliant switch from toms to splashy ride, and the celebrated harmony sixths. The joy and energy of 'She Loves You' is delightful because it's selfless: the third person go-between lyric aims to patch up a lovers' quarrel. It cast The Beatles as true peacemakers long before the less specific 'All You Need Is Love'. If only they made religions as toe-tappingly compassionate as this.

She Loves You

Words & Music by John Lennon & Paul McCartney

Verse 2:
She said you hurt her so
She almost lost her mind
And now she says she knows
You're not the hurting kind
She says she loves you
And you know that can't be bad,
Yes, she loves you
And you know you should be glad.

Verse 3:
You know it's up to you
I think it's only fair
Pride can hurt you too
Apologize to her
Because she loves you
And you know that can't be bad,
Yes, she loves you
And you know you should be glad.

Mr Tambourine Man

Words & Music by Bob Dylan

Moderately

Chorus

Hey! Mis-ter Tam-bour-ine Man play a song for me, I'm not sleep-y and there

is no place I'm go-in' to.___ Hey! Mis-ter Tam-bour-ine Man

play a song for me, in the jin-gle jan-gle morn-in' I'll come fol - low-in'

5° Fine   *Verse*

you.___ 1. Though I know that eve-nin's em-pire has re-turned in-to sand,

(Verses 2, 3 & 4 see block lyric)

van-ished from my hand, left me blind-ly here to stand, but still not sleep-in'!

My wea-ri-ness a-ma-zes me, I'm brand-ed on my feet, I

Play 4° and repeat Chorus to end

have no one to meet, and the an-cient, emp-ty street's too dead for dream-in'.___

(Chorus)

Verse 2:
Take me on a trip upon your magic swirlin' ship
My senses have been stripped, my hands can't feel to grip.
My toes too numb to step, wait only for my boot heels
To be wanderin'
I'm ready to go anywhere, I'm ready for to fade
Into my own parade, cast your dancin' spell my way
I promise to go under it.

(Chorus)

Verse 3:
Though you might hear laughin' spinnin' swingin' madly across the sun
It's not aimed at anyone, it's just escapin' on the run.
And but for the sky, there are no fences facin'
And if you hear vague traces of skippin' reels of rhyme
To your tambourine in time, it's just a ragged clown behind.
I wouldn't pay it any mind, it's just a shadow you're
Seein' that he's chasin'.

(Chorus)

Verse 4:
Then take me disappearin' through the smoke rings of my mind
Down the foggy ruins of time, far past the frozen leaves
The haunted, frightened trees, out to the windy beach
Far from the twisted reach of crazy sorrow.
Yes, to dance beneath the diamond sky with one hand wavin' free
Silhouetted by the sea, circled by the circus sands
With all memory and fate driven deep beneath the waves
Let me forget about today until tomorrow.

(Chorus)

Mr Tambourine Man

The Byrds

1965 – UK: 1; US: 1

Songs don't come much more pivotal than this. A definitive Dylan cover, 'Mr Tambourine Man' launched The Byrds, popularised the electric 12-string, invented folk-rock and hell... even though this is 1965 you can already feel the West Coast breeze of the Summer of Love blowing through it. The Byrds jettison most of Dylan's verses, regularise the chord-changes and simplify the structure. They start with a chorus, put four verses in the middle and then a chorus to finish. The slower tempo allows Roger McGuinn space for a wonderful laconic vocal which evokes Dylan's patented snarl on the line 'I... promise to go wandering'.

It doesn't have the emotional depth of 'Turn Turn Turn' but the lazy, stoned feel suited the times. The central figure of the lyric is a sort of cross between the Pied Piper and Johnny B. Goode in hippy gear. All the while McGuinn is weaving folk-rock poetry on his Rickenbacker 12-string. 'Mr Tambourine Man' has one of the most memorable chiming guitar intros ever and is a buskers' favourite owing to its three-chord simplicity. Even if you couldn't get the picking exact it sounded okay just strummed. The 12-string sound was indebted to George Harrison's high-profile use of the instrument in *A Hard Day's Night*. The sonic jingle-jangle of 'Mr Tambourine Man' has echoed ever since down the halls of pop to Eighties acts like The Smiths and R.E.M.

The Beatles arrive at Buckingham Palace to receive their MBE awards. They later claimed to have smoked a joint in the royal lavatories prior to their investiture.

Five years later John Lennon returned his MBE as a "protest against the Vietnam war and 'Cold Turkey' dropping down the UK charts".

Yesterday

The Beatles
1965 – US: 1; 1976 – UK: 8

So let me introduce to you...the most-covered song of all-time with over 2,500 versions. It's not difficult to hear why. Musically 'Yesterday' is as elegant as anything The Beatles ever recorded, with McCartney's strummed, detuned acoustic (the key is F major but he plays an open G chord) supported by a string quartet. McCartney was suspicious of putting strings on 'Yesterday', fearing the result would be too MOR but it worked. In stark contrast to more recent ballads, there's plenty of harmonic change.

Notice how within the first few bars the song slides away from its home key into the relative minor. 'Yesterday' stands as welcoming to interpretation as the Statue of Liberty. It's a simple expression of regret. The messy but life-like details which occur in other McCartney love songs of the time like 'You Won't See Me' are banished. She's gone, he doesn't know why and he's miserable. Her inexplicable leaving is at once the song's heart of fudge (pun intended) and a reason for its popularity. No-one gets blamed, the buck stops nowhere... unless maybe with the strings. For this reason 'Yesterday' has a curiously dead air of perfection, the regret stuck like an insect

trapped in amber, in contrast to the sharper, explicit tensions of a song like 'In My Life'. But this is not to imply the old chestnut about tough man Lennon versus sweet boy McCartney. In 1999 pop music needs to re-learn the melodic grace of McCartney's best work, a grace 'Yesterday' has in spades.

'Yesterday' wasn't released as a single in the UK during The Beatles' collective career because the group felt it would send the wrong message to fans. They were a rock'n'roll group first and foremost.

Yesterday

Words & Music by John Lennon & Paul McCartney

Moderately, with expression

Good Vibrations

Words & Music by Brian Wilson & Mike Love

Verse 2:
Close my eyes, she's somehow closer now
Softly smile, I know she must be kind.
Then I look in her eyes
She goes with me to a blossom world.

The queen of 'Op Art' Bridget Riley photographed in 1966 in front of one of her visually vibrating abstract paintings. Her work was a strong influence on both pop fashion and design.

Good Vibrations

The Beach Boys
1966 – UK: 1; US: 1

'Good Vibrations' is at once the first hint of the sun setting on Brian Wilson's genius and a glimmer of the dawn of the Summer of Love. Lyrically, it's a hippy take on 'The Girl From Ipanema'. Brian Wilson used whole careers of studio time to obsessively set and re-set the basic musical ideas, and the final version links parts taken from many takes. The assemblage is apparent in the abrupt transitions and audible changes in recording tone. As a consequence 'Good Vibrations' is hugely ambitious and delightfully unpredictable but perhaps falls short of the melodic and structural perfection of 'God Only Knows'.

Among many Beach Boy records, like 'Don't Worry Baby', 'I Get Around', 'Wouldn't It Be Nice', and 'Darlin'', which demand a place in any selection of songs from the era, 'Good Vibrations' stands out for the sheer ground-breaking quality of its sound. It combines the space-age whoop of a theremin, The Beach Boys' blue ozone-filled harmonies, a driving cello, high bass guitar arpeggios, on the beat keyboard chords (a favourite Wilson motif) and an organ that brings a religious intensity to the love experience, and does it all in three minutes 35 seconds which at the time was considered enormously long. The result is a pocket symphony whose melodic invention was and remains something quite outside the reach of most pop writers.

Strawberry Fields Forever

Words & Music by John Lennon & Paul McCartney

Let me take you down, 'cause I'm go-in' to Straw-ber-ry Fields, no-thing is real, and no-thing to get hung a-bout,

John Lennon on location in Spain for Richard Lester's film How I Won The War. *It was here that he wrote 'Strawberry Fields Forever'.*

Strawberry Fields Forever
The Beatles
1967 – UK: 2; US: 8
The greatest double-sided single of all time (the flip was 'Penny Lane'), 'Strawberry Fields' is an intensely personal song that perfectly defined its era. The psychedelic scene in England often drew on images of childhood, and the Englishness is felt in the harpsichord and cellos, which mix with sound-effects and backward cymbals. Lennon's vision required technical wizardry to be realised. His voice is slurred through vari-speeding and he insisted that the first part of one take be welded on to another. One take was slowed down and the other speeded up until they matched, which left the song pitched between B♭ and A. This dislocation fits the psychic dislocation which imbues the lyric, with its strange hesitancies ('no, I mean, a yes') and images. Twice in each verse it sounds as though the F♯ chord is about to take us into a new key only to fall back to D each time. The melody is far more angular than is usual with Lennon.

The opening mellotron flutes and first line 'Let me take you down' will continue to have a dizzying effect on people of a certain age and or imagination. This is not just a time tunnel to the heady days of 1967 but to somewhere even further back, a lost idealised childhood, where 'no-one I think is in my tree'.

Ironically, The Beatles' double-sided slab of genius failed to reach number one in the UK, thus breaking a run of chart toppers that went all the way back to 'Please Please Me'. Shamefully, Elgelbert Humperdinck's vacuous ballad 'Release Me' stubbornly refused to make way for 'Penny Lane'/'Strawberry Fields Forever'.

Verse 2:
No one I think is in my tree
I mean it must be high or low.
That is, you know you can't tune in
But it's all right
That is, I think it's not too bad.

Verse 3:
Always know sometimes, think it's me
But you know I know when it's a dream.
I think I know of thee, ah yes
But it's all wrong
That is, I think I disagree.

Love Is All Around
The Troggs
1967 – UK: 6; US: 7

Hailing from Wiltshire, The Troggs are remembered for a small run of Sixties pop hits including 'Wild Thing', famously torched by Jimi Hendrix at Monterey and thereafter associated as much with him as the band who wrote it. News of the Summer of Love was obviously a bit late getting down to Wiltshire as 'Love Is All Around' didn't chart until the end of 1967 in the UK and the following year in the US. In The Troggs' hands it was a charmingly shambolic slice of naive English pop, all straw-chewing innocence and out-of-tune guitars, which Reg Presley claimed he wrote in 15 minutes. The chord sequence is a corker: I-II-IV-V, the same that fuelled R.E.M's 'Fall On Me' (1986) and Maria McKee's 'Show Me Heaven' (1990). Ironically with their penchant for Sixties obscurities, R.E.M. actually took to performing it in concert. Perhaps as a consequence, in the Nineties Wet Wet Wet took the song, removed the straw and flowers of 1967, tuned the guitars, and went to number one with a spruced up version. Of course, its inclusion in the smash-hit movie *Four Weddings And A Funeral* helped a bit.

Another wet Sunday in 1967's Summer of Love. Yet another Carnaby Street sign is liberated.

Following pages Mods and the Mini, the very essence of the mid-Sixties.

Love Is All Around

Words & Music by Reg Presley

Verse 2:
I see your face before me
As I lay on my bed;
I cannot get to thinking
Of all the things you said.

You gave your promise to me
And I gave mine to you;
I need someone beside me
In everything I do.

All Along The Watchtower

Words & Music by Bob Dylan

Moderately

"There must be some way out— of here", said the jok-er to the thief,

"There's too much— con - fu - sion, I can't get no re - lief."—

Hendrix increased the guitar's sonic vocabulary more than anyone before... the century's most expressive rock guitar virtuoso.

All Along The Watchtower
Jimi Hendrix
1968 - UK: 5; US: 20
Sometimes it's the way an artist covers a song that reveals their stature. The more famous the original, the greater the feat if you make a song yours forever. Hendrix's 'All Along The Watchtower' has eclipsed Dylan's acoustic original on *John Wesley Harding*. A big Dylan fan, Hendrix sensed untold elements within the song's mysterious, apocalyptic lyric. It's musically simple, though Hendrix's version has two more chords than people think. Mitchell's drum opening is explosive, and Dave Mason contributes a ghostly 12-string rhythm, underneath which Hendrix plays a soulful syncopated bass-line. Though generally perceived as a rock number, 'Watchtower' has a strong soul element. Few rock songs groove like this.

In 1968 Hendrix was the un-disputed champ of rock guitar. He'd done things with the instrument no-one thought possible. But his virtuosity wasn't always able to find material big enough for it. In 'Watchtower' the guitar-playing rises to the emotional power of the song. He plays superb lead, including a masterpiece triple-punch break going from slide to wah-wah to trebly chords. All this makes the song visual. This version is to Dylan's what a flickering b/w 8mm film is to colour cinemascope. The whole thing sweeps into grandeur as he sings of the riders approach-ing and the wind beginning to howl... showing in wide-screen format from a pair of head-phones near you.

U2 included a version of the song in their *Rattle And Hum* movie and did their best to emulate the soaring heights of Hendrix's version in concert.

"Bus-'ness men,— they drink my wine,— plow-men— dig my earth.

None of them a - long the line,— know what a-ny of it is worth."—

"No rea-son to get ex-ci - ted," the thief, he kind-ly spoke,—

"There are ma-ny here a-mong us, who feel that life is but a joke.

But you and I, we've been thru that, and this is not our fate.—

So let us not talk false-ly now, the hour is get-ting late."—

All a-long the watch-tow-er,— Prin-ces kept the view,—

while all the wo-men came and went, bare-foot ser-vants too.—

Out - side— in the dis-tance, a wild-cat did growl.—

Two ri-ders were ap-proach-ing, the wind be-gan to howl.

My Way
Frank Sinatra
1969 – UK: 5; US: 27
First published in 1967, the English lyrics of 'My Way' were written by Paul Anka to an existing French tune by Jacques Revaux. Interestingly, David Bowie was also invited to compose lyrics to the song but his efforts were rejected by the publishers.

Frank Sinatra first recorded the song in 1969 and it became the anthem of his "Ol' Blue Eyes Is Back" years, including the 'Main Event' tour, TV special and album in 1974. It was a big theatrical song to mark his transition from intimate saloon singer to stadium performer. Audience's identified the song's defiant bravado with Sinatra's own turbulent life. Will Friedwald: "The message cemented Sinatra's profile as a mythic figure in American culture, someone who had faced impossible odds and been very nearly beaten, yet underwent a heroic transformation and was born anew."

Sinatra later came to dislike singing what he jokingly called "the second National Anthem" but although he had been identified with many other songs over his long career, notably 'Strangers In the Night', this is the one that now defines Ol' Blue Eyes for all time.

Naturally enough, 'My Way' has been recorded by dozens of other artists, including such disparate names as Elvis Presley and The Sex Pistols. Sinatra's version spent a total of 122 weeks on the British charts.

July 20, 1969:
Neil Armstrong's first
footprint on the Moon.

My Way

Words & Music by Claude Francois, Jacques Revaux & Gilles Thibaut
English words by Paul Anka

Verse 2:
Regrets, I've had a few
But then again too few to mention.
I did what I had to do
And saw it through without exemption.
I planned each chartered course
Each careful step along the by-way.
And more, much more than this
I did it my way.

Yes there were times, I'm sure you knew
When I bit off more than I could chew.
But through it all when there was doubt
I ate it up and spit it out.
I faced it all and I stood tall
And did it my way.

Verse 3:
I've loved, I've laughed and cried
I've had my fill, my share of losing.
And now as tears subside
I find it all so amusing.
To think, I did all that
And may I say, not in a shy way.
Oh no, oh no not me
I did it my way.

For what is a man, what has he got
If not himself, then he has not.
To say the things he'd truly feel
And not the words of one who kneels
The record shows, I took the blows
And did it my way.

Give Peace A Chance

Words & Music by John Lennon & Paul McCartney

Moderately

1. Ev - 'ry - bo - dy's talk - ing a - bout Bag - is - m, Shag - is - m, Drag - is - m, Mad - is - m,
(Verses 2, 3 & 4 see block lyric)

Rag - is - m, Tag - is - m, This - is - m, That - is - m, is - n't it the most.

All we — are say - - ing _____ is give peace a chance.

_____ All we — are say - - ing _____ is

give peace a chance. _____

1. C'mon. **2.** Let me tell you now.

3. Oh let's stick to it. **4.** All we — are say - - ing _____ is

give peace — a chance. _____ *Repeat ad lib. to fade* All we are

Verse 2:
Everybody's talking about
Ministers, Sinisters
Banisters and Canisters
Bishops and Fishops
Rabbis and Popeyes
Bye bye, bye byes.

Verse 3:
Everybody's talking about
Revolution, Evolution
Mastication, Flagellation
Regulations, Integrations
Meditations, United Nations
Congratulations.

Verse 4:
Everybody's talking about
John and Yoko, Timmy Leary
Rosemary, Tommy Smothers
Bobby Dylan, Tommy Cooper
Derek Taylor, Norman Mailer
Alan Ginsberg, Hare Krishna, Hare, Hare Krishna.

Give Peace A Chance

John Lennon

1969 – UK: 1; US: 14

John Lennon would have made a great headline writer. He had a rare talent for coining a memorable phrase that became a song, and in this case it also became the universal anthem of the international peace movement whose canonisation in this regard is unlikely ever to be challenged. 'Give Peace A Chance' has been sung at peace rallies ever since it was recorded somewhat casually in a Montreal hotel room during one of John and Yoko's bed-ins for peace in 1969.

"I was pleased when the movement in America took up 'Give Peace A Chance', " Lennon explained, "because I had written it with that in mind really. I hoped that instead of singing 'We Shall Overcome', they would have something contemporary. I felt an obligation, even then, to write a song that people would sing in a pub or on a demonstration." Today, this all-purpose chant is still used by all sorts of pressure groups and is not only sung in pubs but on football terraces, where the familiar refrain "All we are saying is give us a goal" echoes through television and radio commentaries.

Credited to The Plastic Ono Band, the exuberant record also features the vocal talents of Yoko, Abbie Hoffman, Timothy Leary, Tommy Smothers, Murray The K, Derek Taylor, several peace-loving clerics and a group from the Radha Krishna Temple. Although the recording gives the impression of having been recorded spontaneously, Lennon did return to the studio and add vocal overdubs and Ringo Starr on drums.

John and Yoko Lennon at the Toronto Hilton during their 'Bed-In' for world peace. Here they recorded 'Give Peace A Chance' with various celebrity backing vocalists.

Woodstock

1970 – UK: 1; US: 11
UK: Matthews Southern Comfort
US: Crosby, Stills, Nash & Young

The end of the Sixties saw the rise of the rock festival, great tribal gatherings of free-spirited rock fans who assembled in fields to hear the supergroups of the day, often in atrocious sanitary conditions while the rain poured from the skies. Of all the great festivals, none has passed into legend more than Woodstock, a largely spontaneous gathering of anything up to half-a-million US fans who made their way to the town of Bethel in upstate New York over the weekend of August 15-17, 1969. Among the performers were The Grateful Dead, The Who, Jimi Hendrix, The Band, Joe Cocker and Santana. Making only their second appearance that day with Neil Young as part of the group were Crosby, Stills, Nash

and Young who would record Joni Mitchell's paen to those who gathered that day on *Deja Vue*, their first LP as a quartet.

Mitchell wrote the song because she was prevented from going to Woodstock, largely because there was no room on the helicopter and she had a TV engagement on the same day. Watching the TV coverage in her hotel room, she was so moved that she sat down and wrote this song. Stephen Stills was actually in the process of writing his own song about the festival but when Joni showed him her song, he abandoned the task. "I can't top that," he said. CSN&Y then recorded their searing electric version of Joni Mitchell's ballad.

Matthews Southern Comfort, led by former Fairport Conventioner Ian Matthews, recorded a version closer to Joni's original which went to the top of the UK charts.

Half a million people, almost all aged between 15 and 25, gather at a rented 600-acre dairy farm near Woodstock, New York, in the rain and wind to listen to three days of music.

Woodstock

Words & Music by Joni Mitchell

Slow Folk style

1. I came up on a child of God, he was walk-ing a long the
(Verses 2 & 3 see block lyric)
road and I asked him, "Where are you go - ing?" This he told me:
"I'm go-ing on down to Yas - gur's Farm, gon-na join in a rock and roll
band. I'm gon-na camp out on the land, and try 'n' get my soul
free." We are star - dust, we are
gold - en. And we got to get our - selves back to the
gar - - - - - den. 2. "Then
caught in the de - vil's bar - gain and we got to get our - selves
back to the gar - - - - - - den.

Verse 2:
"Then can I walk beside you?
I have come here to lose the smog
And I feel to be a cog in something turning.
Maybe it is just the time of year
Or maybe it's the time of man.
I don't know who I am
But life is for learning."

Verse 3:
By the time we got to Woodstock
We were half a million strong
And ev'rywhere was song and celebration.
And I dreamed I saw the bombers
Riding shotgun in the sky
Turning into butterflies above our nation.

Chorus 3°
We are stardust
Three billion year old carbon
Caught in the devil's bargain
And we got to get ourselves
Back to the garden.

Bridge Over Troubled Water

Words & Music by Paul Simon

Verse 2:
When you're down and out
When you're on the street
When evening falls so hard
I will comfort you
I'll take your part
Oh, when darkness comes
And pain is all around.

Verse 3:
Sail on silver girl
Sail on by
Your time has come to shine
All your dreams are on their way
See how they shine
Oh, if you need a friend
I'm sailing right behind.

Bridge Over Troubled Water

Simon & Garfunkel
1970 – UK: 1; US: 1

Simon & Garfunkel's *Bridge Over Troubled Water* album was massively successful (it even outsold *Led Zeppelin II*) but uneven, despite the presence of its stately title track, 'Cecilia' and 'The Boxer', perhaps Simon's best song from the S&G era. 'Bridge Over Troubled Water' itself has hymn-like qualities which stem from Simon's recollection of The Swan Silvertones' 'O Mary Don't You Weep' wherein Claude Jeter sings 'I'll be your bridge over deep water if you trust in My Name'. The echoing production has Art's voice fluttering around like a castrati version of The Righteous Brothers. It's a pretty melody and a dramatic arrangement to boot. The bass line has more bubble than you remember, the percussion goes off like distant gunshots, the strings soar and eventually flood the piano.

Simon and Garfunkel were The Everly Brothers of the Sixties. They wrote a number of fine songs, among them 'Mrs Robinson', the soaring 'America' and 'The Sound Of Silence', their first ever hit. In many ways the *Bridge Over Troubled Water* album became an icon of its era, its dull blue-grey cover and washed out picture of Simon & Garfunkel suggesting the doom and gloom that must surely follow the end of the 20th Century's most colourful decade. So many homes had a copy of this album that its songs became as well known as classics by The Beatles.

There have been over 50 cover versions of 'Bridge Over Troubled Water' by such disparate artists as Elvis Presley, The Jackson 5, Perry Como, Lena Martell and Willie Nelson, not to mention a slew of male voice choirs.

Simon and Garfunkel were the most successful duo of the Sixties, but their partnership could not survive the success of the Bridge Over Troubled Water *album. Art went into movies and ballads while Paul became one of the century's most respected singer-songwriters.*

*John Lennon performs
'Imagine' at his home studio
at Tittenhurst Park. Each
recording session there was
filmed and some sequences
were later included in the
Imagine film.*

Imagine
*John Lennon
1971 – US: 3; 1975: UK: 6;
1980: UK: 1*
John Lennon was a rocker at
heart and a world class one at
that, so it seems a bit ironic that
his best known song 'Imagine' is
a tender, melodic ballad. But
'Imagine' has a hymn-like
quality which preached peace
and unselfishness in a simple
language the whole world could
understand, and it stands as a
wonderful memorial to The
Beatles' guiding light and
artistic conscience. The lyrics to
'Imagine' were inspired by
Yoko Ono's book *Grapefruit*, but
the essence of the song was pure
Lennon, a moving anthem that
has come to define the innocent
hope for world peace that John
propagated during the latter
part of his life.

In America, the song proved
successful as a single, reaching
number three, but in the UK it
was played only as a track from
the album of the same name
until its belated release in 1975.
It was not until after Lennon's
murder that 'Imagine' climbed
to number one in the UK. By
this time it had become
something of a standard.

The Utopean idealism of
'Imagine' attracted criticism,
not least because Lennon
seemed to be propagating a
kind of communist ideal –
"Imagine no possessions" –
when everyone knew that he
was a wealthy man. Religious
groups were also concerned
about the line "no religion too"
but John had an answer for
them: "If you can imagine a
world at peace, with no
denominations of religion – not
without religion, but without
this 'my God is bigger than your
God' thing – then it can be
true."

Imagine

Words & Music by John Lennon

Verse 3:

Imagine no possessions
I wonder if you can.
No need for greed or hunger
A brotherhood of man.
Imagine all the people
Sharing all the world.

You, you may say I'm a dreamer
But I'm not the only one.
I hope some day you will join us
And the world will live as one.

Amazing Grace

Traditional

Moderately

1. A - maz - ing grace! How sweet the sound that
(Verse 2 see block lyric)

saved a wretch like me! I once was

lost, but now am found; was blind but now I

see. 'Twas grace that taught my heart to

fear and grace my fears re - lieved. How

pre - cious did that grace ap - pear the hour I

1. first be - lieved! **2.** Through -gun.

Verse 2:
Through many dangers, toils and snares
I have already come
'Tis grace hath brought me safe thus far
And grace will lead me home.
When we've been there ten thousand years
Bright shining as the sun
We've no less days to sing God's praise
Than when we first begun.

One of many, frequent demonstrations around the world against the escalating war in Vietnam, here agianst the invasion of Cambodia. It was not until January 1973 that a Vietnam peace treaty was signed. By the end of March 1973, all US fighting forces had been withdrawn.

Amazing Grace
Judy Collins
1971 – UK: 5; US: 15

Judy Collins started her career as a traditional folk singer but shifted towards contemporary material like Joni Mitchell's 'Both Sides Now' which charted in 1968. Stephen Stills wrote 'Suite: Judy Blue Eyes' for her, and in 1975 she had a hit with 'Send In The Clowns', from the Sondheim musical *A Little Night Music*.

'Amazing Grace' is a traditional tune of 1779 attributed to hymn writer Rev. John Newton, a religious song of quiet dignity and resolute faith, whose melody builds ever upward through each verse. Its lyric carries a plain but profound tale of redemption, summed up in the imagery of 'was blind but now I see'. Collins' a cappella version was recorded at St. Paul's Chapel, Columbia

University. It brought her international success and probably re-established the song itself as a standard.

Rod Stewart sang it memorably to a slide guitar accompaniment on *Every Picture Tells A Story* (1971) and The Royal Scots Dragoon Guards took an instrumental arrangement into the UK charts in 1972.

American Pie

Words & Music by Don McLean

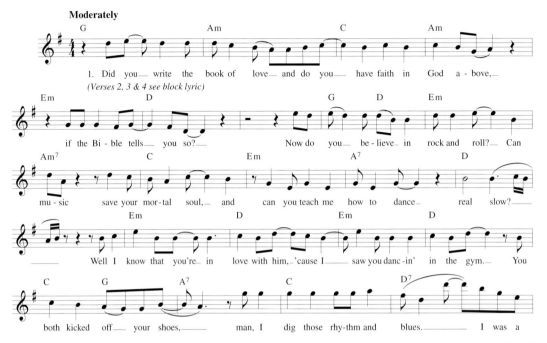

Moderately

1. Did you write the book of love and do you have faith in God a-bove,
(Verses 2, 3 & 4 see block lyric)
if the Bi-ble tells you so? Now do you be-lieve in rock and roll? Can
mu-sic save your mor-tal soul, and can you teach me how to dance real slow?
Well I know that you're in love with him, 'cause I saw you danc-in' in the gym. You
both kicked off your shoes, man, I dig those rhy-thm and blues. I was a

The inauguration of the Boeing 747, the first jumbo jet, in Seattle in 1969.

American Pie

Don McLean
1972 – UK: 2; US: 1

The early Seventies singer-songwriters were earnest young men and women clutching acoustic guitars, singing downbeat songs with self-consciously poetic, 'important' lyrics. Among the best were Tim Hardin, Tim Buckley, James Taylor, Joni Mitchell, Gordon Lightfoot and Neil Young out of CSN. Don McLean is remembered for 'Vincent', a ballad about Van Gogh, and 'American Pie'.

The importance of 'American Pie' was announced by its length (the B-side was Part 2) determined by the lyric. The song had a beat, neat piano and a chord sequence guitar tyros could bash out, but it was the words that counted more than anything. It started – 'a long, long time ago' – as an elegy for the death of Buddy Holly and by implication rock'n'roll. McLean nostalgically evoked a pre-assassination USA of the Fifties, with references to high school gyms, drinking, James Dean, chevys and pickup trucks, and The Monotones' 'The Book Of Love'. The later verses came on like the missing link between Dylan and early Springsteen, an obscure allegory of the turbulent Sixties with jesters, kings, queens, Lennon reading Marx and The Byrds' 'Eight Miles High'. With its singalong chorus replete with exuberant internal rhymes, 'American Pie' ends up partially disproving its own thesis of 'the day the music died'.

lone - ly teen - age bronc - in' buck with a pink car - na - tion and a pick-up truck, but I knew I was out of luck the day the mu - sic died. I start - ed sing - ing. bye - bye Miss A - me - ri - can Pie, drove my Che - vy to the le - vee but the le - vee was dry. Them good old boys were drink - in' whis - ky and rye, sing - in' this - 'll be the day that I die, this - 'll be the day that I die. this - 'll be the day that I die.

Verse 2:
Now for ten years we've been on our own, and moss grows fat on a rollin' stone
But that's not how it used to be when the jester sang for the king and queen
In a coat he borrowed from James Dean and a voice that came from you and me.
Oh and while the king was looking down, the jester stole his thorny crown
The courtroom was adjourned, no verdict was returned.
And while Lenin read a book on Marx the quartet practised in the park
And we sang dirges in the dark
The day the music died.

Verse 3:
Helter-skelter in the summer swelter, the birds flew off with a fallout shelter
Eight miles high and fallin' fast, it landed foul on the grass.
The players tried for a forward pass, with the jester on the sidelines in a cast
Now the half-time air was sweet perfume while the sargeants played a marching tune.
We all got up to dance but we never got the chance
'Cause all the players tried to take the field, the marching band refused to yield.
Do you recall what was revealed
The day the music died.

Verse 4:
And there we were all in one place, a generation lost in space
With no time left to start again.
So come on, Jack be nimble, Jack be quick, Jack Flash sat on a candlestick
'Cause fire is the devil's only friend.
And as I watched him on the stage, my hands were clenched in fists of rage
No angel born in hell could break that Satan's spell.
And as the flames climbed high into the night to light the sacrificial rite
I saw Satan laughing with delight
The day the music died.

Layla

Words & Music by Eric Clapton & Jim Gordon

Moderately, with a beat

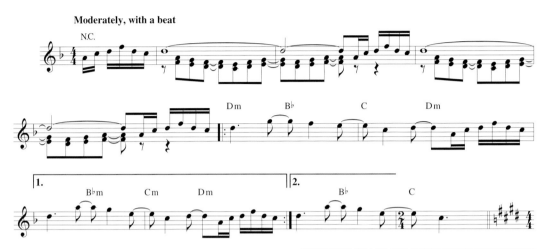

Layla

Derek & The Dominoes
1972 – UK: 7

'Layla' is a definitive moment in rock, a song where rock's musical fire-power is harnessed to something other than youthful rebellion or anger and finds a subject worth its energy. It came from *Layla And Other Assorted Love Songs*, a double album Eric Clapton recorded with friends as Derek & The Dominoes. The guitarist had tired of the 'Clapton Is God' burden he'd carried since Cream and Blind Faith. Angry over the death of Hendrix in September 1970, Clapton was tortured by emotional longing for Patti Harrison, George's wife. (Few women have inspired so many top-flight songs as the former Patti Boyd. George's beautiful 'Something' was also about her.)

'Layla' has a lot going for it: an empathic band performance, fine slide work from Duane Allman, a great ravaged vocal by Clapton, and that riff, with a complementary figure sandwiched between the high and low parts. A simple structure means no middle eight but the contrast of the D minor chorus and the verse hovering between C♯ minor and E is unusual. The single lacks the instrumental coda in C major which takes the song into another dimension. Despite suffering from over-familiarity, when heard afresh the passion of 'Layla' is still startling.

Together, Eric Clapton and 'Layla' arrive at London's Heathrow airport in the mid-Seventies.

Verse 2:
Tried to give you consolation
Your old man won't let you down.
Like a fool, I fell in love with you
Turned the whole world upside down.

Verse 3:
Let's make the best of the situation
Before I finally go insane.
Please don't say we'll never find a way
And tell me all my love's in vain.

*June, 1972: Richard Nixon
was re-elected in 1972 by
one of the largest majorities in
US history, but a small cloud
soon appeared on the horizon.
The attempted burglary and
wiretapping of the Democratic
headquarters at the Watergate
complex was traced to some
of Nixon's closest advisers.
Determined reporting
uncovered illegal campaign
contributions, 'dirty tricks'
and irregularities in Nixon's
income tax. Eventually, on
August 8, 1973 he announced
his resignation, unprecedented
in US history.*

Without You

Harry Nilsson
1972 – UK: 1; US: 1

Few bands in rock history
suffered as tragically as
Badfinger. Enjoying the mixed
blessing of being signed to The
Beatles' Apple label and even
having a McCartney-written hit
'Come And Get It' to launch
their careers, they never quite
fulfilled their promise. By the
mid-Seventies the band had
succumbed to managerial
dissatisfaction, contract
problems and penury.
Despondent over their
misfortune, the writers of
'Without You', Pete Ham and
Tom Evans, committed suicide
in 1975 and 1983 respectively.

Most of those who bought
Nilsson's 'Without You' had
never heard of Badfinger. They
fell for the dynamic contrast of
his version, all plangent piano
chords, heartbroken verses and
wailing choruses. The emotion
was simple and painted in bold
strokes. He can't forget the
evening, she's full of sorrow,
he's full of sorrow, even the
strings are full of sorrow.
Badfinger's recording is a little
harder, quicker, with shades of
The Beatles here and there,
some extra chords and a great
guitar figure on the chorus. It
often falls on deaf ears for those
who come to it after Nilsson's
but Badfinger's 'Without You'
has its own virtues.

Mariah Carey's Nineties
version veered more towards
Nilsson and was a smash hit.
The royalties on this song
should have made Ham and
Evans millionaires.

Without You

Words & Music by Peter Ham & Tom Evans

Candle In The Wind

Words & Music by Elton John & Bernie Taupin

Not too slow

1. Good-bye Nor-ma Jean_____ though I nev-er knew you at all
(Verse 2 see block lyric)
_____ you had_____ the grace to hold your-self_____ while those a-round_____ you crawled.
They crawled out of the wood-work_____ and they whis-pered
in-to_____ your brain_____ they set you on a tread-mill_____ and they

The newlywed Princess of Wales, at the start of her honeymoon with her new husband and her new mother-in-law.

Following pages Diana on stage at the Royal Opera House, dancing with ballet star Wayne Sleep at a charity gala.

Candle In The Wind

Elton John
1974- UK 7; 1997: UK: 1; US: 1

Not all singer-songwriters had acoustic guitars, some had pianos. Elton John arrived in the early Seventies with several albums' worth of catchy pop, moody orchestrated ballads and country-rock with Wild West lyrics courtesy of partner Bernie Taupin. The brilliant match of talents created hugely popular songs like 'Your Song', 'Crocodile Rock', 'Daniel', 'Rocket Man' and 'Goodbye

Yellow Brick Road'. By the mid-Seventies Elton was the biggest solo rock act on the planet.

'Candle In The Wind' began life on his *Goodbye Yellow Brick Road* album as a eulogy to Marilyn Monroe. Addressing her by her real name of Norma Jean was a trick that drew the listener into the young man's wish-fantasy of actually knowing her. A fine narrative lyric by Taupin traces Monroe's rise to stardom and its attendant problems of loneliness and

despair. Elton provides a strong setting and Davey Johnstone a memorable guitar hook.

Although not one of Elton's gigantic hits at the time of release, it was a concert favourite that gained in stature as the years went by, and in the Eighties Elton re-recorded it live with a symphony orchestra, dressed for the concert as Mozart! But its apotheosis was to come with the death of Diana, Princess of Wales, in 1997. Believed to have been one of Diana's favourite songs,

public demand somehow insisted that Elton perform the song during her funeral service in Westminster Abbey and Taupin altered the words for the occasion. The lust and romance of the boy in the twenty-second row were replaced by a Blakeian pastoral fantasy of England's 'rose' walking on green hills, and as a charity record it went on to become the biggest selling single ever.

Verse 2:
Loneliness was tough
The toughest role you ever played
Hollywood created a super star
And pain was the price you paid
Even when you died
Oh the press still hounded you
All the papers had to say
Was that Marilyn was found in the nude.

Packed with British troops, the liner Canberra sails from Portsmouth to the Falkland Islands following their invasion by Argentina.

Sailing
Rod Stewart
1975 – UK: 1,

Rod Stewart was an ex-Mod with a glorious sandpaper voice who loved football, made an album with Jeff Beck, and revered Sam Cooke and David Ruffin. He had a fine eye for Dylan songs, a talent for folk-rock songwriting in an English tradition, and some great pals with whom to record. He made two pretty good solo albums (*An Old Raincoat, Gasoline Alley*), and two excellent solo albums (*Every Picture Tells A Story, Never A Dull Moment*). 'Maggie May' (from *Every Picture*), a UK and US No.1, made him an international star. His band The Faces became a top concert draw of the day, their gigs generating a unique party atmosphere.

He was, quite simply, one of the best rock vocalists the UK ever produced.

'Sailing' is an anthem full of vague yearnings perfectly engineered for mass scarf-waving at stadium concerts where Rod's fans gathered in their thousands. It was designed to appeal to the widest of wide audiences and Rod's version became a sing-along tour-de-force, but compared to 'Mandolin Wind', or the cover of the Motown classic 'I Know I'm Losing You', 'Sailing' is a dinghy to an ocean liner.

'Sailing' was written by Gavin Sutherland, who, with brother Iain as The Sutherland Brothers, teamed with Quiver to produce a 1976 hit with 'Arms Of Mary'.

Sailing

Words & Music by Gavin Sutherland

Slowly

1. I am sail-ing, I am sail-ing, home a-gain 'cross the sea. I am
(Verse 2 see block lyric)

sail-ing stor-my wa-ters, to be near you, to be free. 2. I am

free. 3. Can you hear me, can you hear me, thro' the dark night far a-

-way? I am dy-ing, for-ev-er try-ing, to be

with you, who can say. 4. Can you hear me, can you hear me, thro' the
(Verse 5 see block lyric)

dark night, far a-way? I am dy-ing, for-ev-er

try-ing, to be with you, who can say. 5. We are

free. Oh Lord, to be near you, to be free. Oh Lord, to be

Repeat to fade

Verse 2:
I am flying, I am flying
Like a bird 'cross the sky.
I am flying, passing high clouds
To be with you, to be free.

Verse 5:
We are sailing, we are sailing
Home again 'cross the sea.
We are sailing stormy waters
To be near you, to be free.

No Woman, No Cry

Words & Music by Bob Marley & Vincent Ford

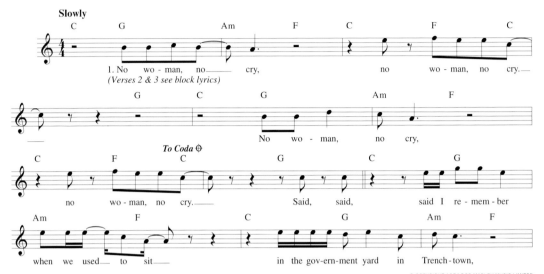

Slowly

1. No wo-man, no— cry, no wo-man, no cry.—
(Verses 2 & 3 see block lyrics)

No wo - man, no cry,

To Coda ⊕

no wo-man, no cry.— Said, said, said I re-mem-ber

when we used— to sit— in the gov-ern-ment yard in Trench-town,

The first international superstar of reggae, Bob Marley checks the quality of some home produce!

No Woman, No Cry
Bob Marley & The Wailers
1975 – UK: 8
Recorded live at the Lyceum in London, an epic moment when band and audience mould as one. In the stale UK music scene of 1975, trapped in the death-agonies of glam, teeny-bopper pop and progressive rock, the ethnicity of 'No Woman, No Cry' stood out like a diamond. Following Clapton's cover of 'I Shot The Sheriff', it elevated Marley to the status of reggae's first world superstar.

This is a song whose greatness is inseparable from its definitive performance. 'No Woman, No Cry' is a song of exile with a strong sense of locality. Marley delivers his reminiscence of the yard in Trenchtown with a passionate vocal. It's about as politically defined as 'Blowin' In The Wind', but it's the humanity that's important. Musically it couldn't be simpler: a four chord sequence of I-V-VI-IV (same as The Police's 'So Lonely' but slower) with no structure of which to speak. There's only slight changes in the arrangement, notably at the exhilirating moment when Marley and the backing singers hit the 'Everything's gonna be alright' line to fiery stabs of organ and the whole thing turns into Jamaican gospel.

Verse 2:
No woman no cry, no woman no cry
Here little darling, don't shed no tears
No woman no cry
Said, said, said I remember when we used to sit
In the government yard in Trenchtown
And the Georgie would make the fire light
As it was log wood burning through the night
Then we would cook corn meal porridge
Of which I'll share with you
Ooh my feet is my only carriage
So I've got to push on say.

Verse 3:
No woman no cry, no no woman no cry
Woman little sister, don't shed no tear
No woman no cry.

I Write The Songs

Words & Music by Bruce Johnston

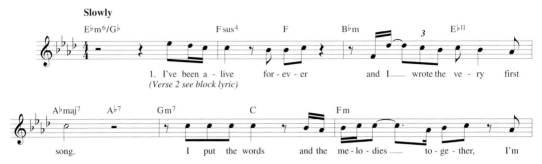

Slowly

E♭m6/G♭   Fsus4   F   B♭m   E♭11

1. I've been a - live   for - ev - er   and I___ wrote the ve - ry   first
(Verse 2 see block lyric)

A♭maj7   A♭7   Gm7   C   Fm

song.   I   put   the   words   and   the   me - lo - dies___   to - ge - ther,   I'm

I Write The Songs

Barry Manilow
1976 – US: 1

Originally a jingle-writer and musical accompanist for the singer Bette Midler, Barry Manilow is sneered at by critics but adored by millions of female fans. His mellifluous tenor and schmaltzy brand of commercial MOR has been enormously successful and among his biggest hits are 'Mandy' (1974), 'Looks Like We Made ' (1977), 'Can't Smile Without You' (1978) and 'Copacabana (At The Copa)' (1978).

He wrote most of his songs himself but his biggest US hit, 'I Write The Songs', was penned by Beach Boy Bruce Johnston. Though critics have suggested that Manilow lacks depth, in the Eighties he collaborated with Gerry Mulligan and Sarah Vaughan on well-received jazz albums. He has also appeared in one-man Broadway shows and turned his song 'Copacabana' into a stage musical.

'I Write The Songs' is the star by sleight-of-hand, celebrating his gift even though he didn't actually write it himself. David Cassidy had a UK hit with it in 1975.

1976 saw the greatest drought in Britain in history. Here is one of the many dried-up reservoirs.

Verse 2:
My home lies deep within you
And I have my own room in your soul.
And we're such good friends
When I look out through your windows
You make me young again
Even though I'm very old.

Mull Of Kintyre

Wings
1977 – UK: 1
Throughout the Seventies Paul
McCartney entertained us with
singles and albums which were
at times pretty good, if not quite
up to the stellar standards of
The Beatles. 'Another Day' was
fine, there was a rude rocker
'Hi Hi Hi' backed by 'C Moon',
both of which were acceptable,
and for the romantics, 'My
Love'. *Band On The Run* was
brilliant. Then there was this.

'Mull Of Kintyre' was a
pick'n'strum tartan waltz with
three chords and a key change
to lift the last verses, and in its
leaps the melody was typical
McCartney. It extolled the
virtues of a remote bit of
Scotland, with heather, sea
mists and so on, all of which was
backed up by on-cue bagpipes.

'Mull Of Kintyre' was a bit of
Tourist Board escapism which
the public loved, and in the
autumn of the 1977, when
Britain was in the grip of a punk
charge led by The Sex Pistols, it
went to number one and
became the biggest selling UK
single to date, eclipsing The
Beatles' 'She Loves You', and
holding the record until Band
Aid released 'Do They Know
It's Christmas' in 1984. Think
what a meal Rod Stewart would
have made of it.

Mull Of Kintyre

Words & Music by Paul McCartney & Denny Laine

Far have I tra-velled and much have I seen, dark dis-tant moun-tains with val-leys of green. Past paint-ed de-serts, the sun-set's on fire as he car-ries me home to the Mull of Kin-tyre.

Mull of Kin-tyre, oh mist roll-ing in from the sea, my de-sire is al-ways to be here, oh Mull of Kin-tyre.

Sweep through the hea-ther like deer in the glen, car-ry me back to the days I knew then. Nights when we sang like a hea-ven-ly choir of the life and the times of the Mull of Kin-tyre.

Mull of Kin-tyre, oh mist roll-ing in from the sea, my de-sire is al-ways to be here, oh Mull of Kin-tyre.

Don't Cry For Me Argentina

Music by Andrew Lloyd Webber
Lyrics by Tim Rice

Slowly

1. It won't be ea - sy, you'll think it strange, when I try to ex - plain how I
(Verses 2 & 3 see block lyric)

feel, that I still need your love af - ter all that I've done: You won't be -

- lieve me, all you will see is a girl you once knew, al - though she's dressed up to the

nines, at six - es and se - vens with you. Don't cry for me Ar - gen -

Slow Tango feel

- ti - na,——— the truth is I ne - ver left you: All through my wild days, my mad ex -

To Coda ✛
poco rall.

D.C. al Coda

- is - tance, I kept my pro - mise, don't keep your dis - tance.——

✛ *Coda*

dis - tance.——— Have I said too much? There's no - thing more I can think of to say to you.

rit.

But all you have to do is look at me to know that ev - 'ry word is true.

(Instrumental)

Verse 2:
I had to let it happen, I had to change
Couldn't stay all my life down at heel
Looking out of the window, staying out of the sun.
So I chose freedom
Running around trying everything new
But nothing impressed me at all
I never expected it to.

Verse 3:
And as for fortune and as for fame
I never invited them in
Though it seemed to the world they were all I desired.
They are illusions
They're not the solutions they promised to be
The answer was here all the time
I love you and hope you love me.

Don't Cry For Me Argentina

Various artists
1977 – UK: 1

Andrew Lloyd Webber and Tim Rice's song from their musical *Evita* is probably the best known from this enormously successful writing partnership. One of a run of successful musicals by Lloyd Webber, including *Jesus Christ Superstar, Cats* and *Phantom Of The Opera, Evita* narrates Eva Peron's rise to fame and death at 33. The lyrics of 'Don't Cry For Me Argentina' are based on a speech she gave at Peron's inauguration on June 4, 1946. Declaring her need for love from the people, Eva Peron talks about freedom to people who have never known the true meaning of the word. From a platform of wealth and privilege come breast-beating platitudes about fame and an ingratiating 'I hope you love me'. This time, she rattles her jewellery and everyone else has to applaud.

Madonna's performance in the 1996 film is arguably better than those by Elaine Paige and Julie Covington, who had a UK number one with it in 1977. The Shadows had a number five with an instrumental version two years later.

A squaddie returns from fighting Argentina in the Falklands Islands.

John Travolta and Karen Lynn Gorney in Saturday Night Fever. Travolta became a new icon for Seventies youth.

Stayin' Alive
The Bee Gees
1978 – UK: 4; US: 1
In the public's mind The Bee Gees are permanently associated with their mid-Seventies renaissance as a disco act, but long before 'Jive Talkin'', 'Tragedy' and their ilk, they recorded a string of memorable Sixties pop hits which didn't feature high voices. These included 'Massachusetts', 'Words' and 'I Gotta Get A Message To You'. Apart from their own global success, they have also written many hit songs for other artists.

In 1974 the brothers found themselves in the extraordinary position of having an album rejected by their label. Changing musical horses brought enormous success and led to the *Saturday Night Fever* phenomenon. The soundtrack yielded three hits – 'How Deep Is Your Love', 'Night Fever', and 'Stayin' Alive' – and was the biggest-selling LP of all time until *Thriller* eclipsed its sales. (It remains the biggest-selling soundtrack.) Sounding like The Chi-Lites on helium, their reedy multi-tracked falsettos delivered a message of dogged survival in the modern city, complete with a steady drum beat, flickers of brass, a single note guitar line, and that gasping chorus, 'ah... ah... ah... ah'. Long after disco, the high voices remain as a trademark on 1987's 'You Win Again', and as the century comes to a close The Bee Gees are enjoying yet another renaissance, their popularity higher than ever.

Stayin' Alive

Words & Music by Barry Gibb, Robin Gibb & Maurice Gibb

Medium rock beat

1. Well, you can tell — by the way I use — my walk, I'm a wo - man's man, no time to talk. —
(Verse 2. see block lyric)

Mu-sic loud and wo - men warm, I've been kicked a -round since I — was born. And now it's all right, — it's o - kay, — and

you may look — the oth - er way. — We can try — to un-der - stand — the New York Times' ef-fect — on man. —

Whe - ther you're a bro-ther or whe - ther you're a mo-ther, you're stay - in' a -live, — stay-in' a - live. —

Feel the ci - ty break-in' and ev - 'ry-bo-dy shak-in' and we're stay-in' a - live, — stay-in' a - live. —

Ah, ha, ha, ha, stay-in' a-live, — stay-in' a - live. — Ah, ha, ha, ha, stay-in' a - live. —

2. Well now, I —

Life go-in' no - where. — Some-bo-dy help me, — some-bo-dy help — me, yeah. —

Life go - in' no - where. — Some - bo - dy help — me, yeah. —

Repeat to fade

I'm stay-in' a - live. —

Verse 2:
Well now, I get low and I get high
And if I can't get either, I really try.
Got the wings of heaven on my shoes
I'm a dancing man and I just can't lose.

You know it's all right, it's okay
I'll live to see another day.
We can try to understand
The New York Times' effect on man.

I Will Survive

Words & Music by Dino Fekaris & Freddie Perren

Solid Beat
(Freely 1st time)

Am   Dm   G

1. At first I was a-fraid, I was pe-tri-fied, kept think-ing I could ne-ver live with-out you
(Verse 2 see block lyric)

Cmaj7   Fmaj7   Bm7(b5)   Esus4

by my side; but then I spent so ma-ny nights think-in' how you did me wrong and I grew strong, and I learned

E   *(A Tempo)* Am   Dm   G

how to get a-long and so you're back from out-er space, I just walked in-to find you here with that sad

Cmaj7   Fmaj7   Bm7(b5)

look up-on your face, I should have changed that stu-pid lock, I should have made you leave your key, if I'd have known

Esus4   E   Am

for just one se-cond you'd be back to bo-ther me. Go on now go, walk out the door,

Dm   G   Cmaj7   Fmaj7

just turn a-round now, ('cause) you're not wel-come a-ny-more. Weren't you the one who tried to hurt

Bm7(b5)   Esus4   E   Am

me with good-bye, did I crum-ble, did you think I'd lay down and die? Oh no, not I. I will sur-vive,

Dm   G   Cmaj7   Fmaj7

oh as long as I know how to love, I know I'll stay a-live: I've got all my life to live, I've got

Bm7(b5)   Esus4   **To Coda** E   Am   Dm   G

all my love to give, and I'll sur-vive, I will sur-vive, hey hey.

D.%. al Coda   Cmaj7   Fmaj7   Bm7(b5)   Esus4   E7

2. It took

Coda   E   Am   Dm   Am

I'll sur-vive.

Verse 2:
It took all the strength I had not to fall apart
Kept tryin' hard to mend the pieces of my broken heart.
And I spent oh so many nights just feelin' sorry for myself
I used to cry, but now I hold my head up high.

And you see me, somebody new
I'm not that chained up little person still in love with you.
And so you feel like droppin' in and just expect me to be free
Now I'm savin' all my lovin' for someone who's lovin' me.

I Will Survive

Gloria Gaynor
1979 – UK: 1; US: 1

Written by Dino Fekaris and
Freddie Perren, 'I Will Survive'
is a typical disco record of its
era which perfectly reflects the
musical and social changes of
the times. Lyrically, it shows in
its own way the revolution in
women's thinking about
relationships. In a Sixties
Motown dance record, Diana
Ross & The Supremes might
have lamented their
powerlessness as 'he' keeps
them hanging on, but Gloria is
having none of that. In 'I Will
Survive' the plot is that 'he'
walked out and left her, and
when he turns up one day to
carry on as if nothing
happened, there's a surprise in
store. 'Uh-uh,' says Gloria,
wagging her head and showing
him the door in no uncertain
terms. Such resolute self-
determination has not been lost
on minorities, which probably
explains why 'I Will Survive'
has become a favourite with gay
men.

If that was a change for the
better, it wasn't necessarily the
same with the music. 'I Will
Survive' is typical of Seventies'
disco in its construction and
rhythm, and far cruder than
comparable Sixties dance
music. The song is an eight-bar
sequence repeated over and
over, with one brief out-of-
tempo lull toward the end.
There's nothing sensual in this
rhythm. That annoying off-beat
hi-hat just rattles on. You can
feel the sweaty touch of the
materialistic Eighties
throughout 'I Will Survive'.
With its air of self-display and
assertion we're one step away
from the aerobic work-out.

*Disco brought with it some of
the worst fashion excesses of
the Seventies, to be seen nightly
in London at venues such as
Stringfellows, seen here.
In New York, the zenith of
disco hedonism was on show
at Studio 54.*

Message In A Bottle

Words & Music by Sting

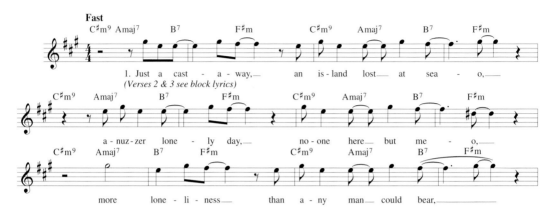

Fast

1. Just a cast - a - way,— an is - land lost— at sea - o,
(Verses 2 & 3 see block lyrics)

a - nuz - zer lone - ly day,— no - one here— but me - o,—

more lone - li - ness— than a - ny man— could bear,—

A state-of-the-art 1978 Bulgarian 'multi panel computer system for preparing data on magnetic tape'.

Message In A Bottle
The Police
1979 – UK: 1

Among the new-wave bands of the late Seventies, The Police were older and wiser than their zippered togs, short hair and urban photo-shoots suggested. The critics dismissed them as 'white reggae', which meant they had rhythmic imagination. They also had plenty of experience, a guitarist intent on a new clean tone and a handsome singer with a striking high voice. They hit first with the slashing chords of 'Roxanne' and the frantic tempo-switches of 'So Lonely', and then showed an exquisite grasp of texture with 'Walking On The Moon'.

'Message In A Bottle' was the first indication The Police were going to be huge. The verse had that off-kilter rhythm they were perfecting and a Summers riff that made a generation of guitarists' fingers ache. A fierce snare hit from Copeland ushered in a chorus whose Cochranesque piledriving abruptly gave way to an elegant, unexpected minor chord and a bunch of harmonics that floated into the ether. Meanwhile Sting had a lyric with a cunning twist in the tale. The 17th Century divine John Donne wrote 'no man is an island', but Sting sang, 'I hope that someone gets my message in a bottle'. A lonely castaway, he wakes up to find not one but a hundred million bottles come ashore. The Police had articulated Man's existential plight and, hey, you could dance to it!

Verse 2:
A year has passed since I wrote my note
But I should have known this right from the start
Only hope can keep me together
Love can mend your life
But love can break your heart.

Verse 3:
Walked out this morning
I don't believe what I saw
A hundred billion bottles washed up on the shore
Seems like I'm not alone in being alone
A hundred billion castaways looking for a home.

December 14, 1980: Times Square, New York. Meanwhile one million people were gathered in Central Park near John Lennon's home, The Dakota, the site of his murder just days earlier.

Woman

John Lennon
1981 – UK: 1; US: 2

After the fine agit-pop of 'Instant Karma', 'Power To The People' and 'Give Peace A Chance' in the early Seventies, John Lennon's muse began to fail. He lacked the creative environment that The Beatles at their best had provided and a suitable creative sparring partner to work against. He was on his own, carrying that weight, writing with an acoustic guitar and a drum machine. 'Woman' came from *Double Fantasy* and went to the top on the wave of popular feeling that followed his appalling death in December 1980.

'Woman' is a well-intentioned confession of male sin and subsequent guilt at his behaviour toward his partner. It moves round predictable changes before rising to a chorus based on a variant of early Sixties pop tunes. There was nothing wrong with the theme but it needed a more imaginative expression. Lennon had lost his invention and the astringency which had made his earlier paeans to Yoko both disturbing and imaginative. The certitude and calm of mature, fulfilled love is a notoriously difficult emotion to express, and in this respect perhaps it's unkind to put 'Woman' up against McCartney's sublime 'Maybe I'm Amazed', which showed how it could be done.

Woman

Words & Music by John Lennon

Verse 2:
Woman I know you understand
The little child inside the man
Please remember, my life is in your hands
And woman hold me close to your heart
However distant, don't keep us apart
After all, it is written in the stars.

Thank You For The Music

Words & Music by Benny Andersson & Björn Ulvaeus

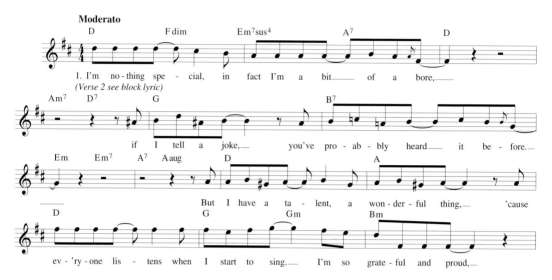

Moderato

1. I'm no-thing spe - cial, in fact I'm a bit___ of a bore,___
(Verse 2 see block lyric)

if I tell a joke, you've pro-ab-bly heard___ it be - fore.

But I have a ta - lent, a won-der - ful thing,___ 'cause

ev - 'ry-one lis - tens when I start to sing.___ I'm so grate-ful and proud,___

Thank You For The Music
Abba
1983 – UK: 33

After their 1974 Eurovision triumph with 'Waterloo', Abba turned into that rare phenomenon: a global band from outside pop's Anglo-American landscape. In the process they became at once the jewel and crown of Eurodisco and single-handedly made a significant impact on Sweden's balance of payments. The infectious quality of their best singles left most of the Top Forty competition standing. Songs like 'S.O.S.', 'Knowing Me, Knowing You', 'The Name Of The Game' and 'The Winner Takes It All' were mini kitchen-sink dramas stuffed with ideas. Abba wrote verses, bridges and choruses so good you were never sure which was which. And of course they recorded the sublime 'Dancing Queen', quite possibly the greatest disco record ever.

'Thank You For The Music' was Abba's symbolic farewell tune, rather like The Supremes' 'Some Day We'll Be Together'. With its tempo fluctuations, mass-voiced chorus, and touching chord changes, it was a gracious gesture as the curtain fell, and was memorably revived by a posse of young Nineties acts at the 1999 Brit Awards. "We thank Abba for the music," sang Bewitched, Steps and friends in a fitting tribute to a style of music that is never really fashionable but, at the same time, never really unfashionable either.

Abba photographed at the height of their fame. Their name derived from the initial letters of their four first names... Agnetha, Bjorn, Benny and Anni-Frid

all I want — is to sing — it out loud. — So I say

thank-you for the mu - sic, the songs I'm sing-ing, thanks for all the joy I'm bring-ing.

Who can live with-out it? I ask in all ho - ne - sty. — What would life be — with-out a song

— or dance, — what are we? So I say thank-you for the mu - sic, for

giv - ing it to me. —

I've been so luc - ky, I am the girl — with gold - en hair, I wan - na sing

it out — to ev - 'ry - bo - dy, what a joy, what a life, what a chance. —

So I say thank-you for the mu - sic, for giv - ing it to me.

Verse 2:
Mother says I was a dancer before I could walk
She says I began to sing long before I could talk
And I've often wondered, how did it start
Who found out that nothing can capture a heart like a melody can?
Well whoever it was, I'm a fan.

In the mid-Eighties the 'New Romantics' regarded appearance more important than their music. Boy George of Culture Club was at the centre of this androgynous movement.

Karma Chameleon

Culture Club
1983 – UK: 1; US: 1

The New Romantics arrived on the coat-tails of the New Wave which in turn fed off the ashes of punk. As much emphasis was placed on the way they dressed as the songs they sang, and it's probably fair to say that the members of both Duran Duran and Spandau Ballet all cringe as they turn the pages of their photo albums, circa 1983. Boy George, the face of Culture Club, went even further, cross-dressing and topping himself off with hats that wouldn't have been out of place at Royal Ascot.

Culture Club came to fame in 1982 with a lightweight piece of white reggae 'Do You Really Want To Hurt Me', fronted by the tubby, good-natured androgyny of singer George. They followed up with a good ballad 'Time' and an acceptable Motown pastiche 'Church Of The Poison Mind'. 'Karma Chameleon' was Culture Club's second number one and final memorable song.

This catchy little ditty became the UK's best-selling single in 1983. How? It's tuneful, it's catchy, it's offensively inoffensive, and has that irritating repetition of 'karma', a word made hip by Lennon. It tries to strike the right poses as George wraps himself up in the Rastafarian flag with the chorus 'red, gold and green' reference.

Karma Chameleon

Words & Music by George O'Dowd, Jonathan Moss, Roy Hay, Michael Craig & Philip Pickett

Verse 2:
Didn't hear your wicked words every day.
And you used to be so sweet I heard you say
That my love was an addiction
When we cling our love is strong.
When you go, you're gone forever
You string along, you string along.

Thriller

Words & Music by Rod Temperton

Moderately bright

1. It's close to mid - night,___ and some-thin' e-vil's lurk-in' in the dark.
(Verses 2 & 3 see block lyrics)

Un - der the moon - light___ you

see a sight that al - most stops your heart.___ You try to scream, but

ter-ror takes the sound be-fore___ you make it.___ You start to freeze___ as

hor-ror looks___ you right___ be - tween the eyes. You're pa - ra - lyzed.___ 'Cause this is

Final touches are applied to Jacko's image for one of his increasingly less frequent public appearances.

Thriller

Michael Jackson
1983 – UK: 11; US: 4

As far as solo vocalists were concerned, the Eighties were dominated by Madonna and three male singers: Springsteen, Prince and Michael Jackson. Jackson's musical career began as a child prodigy in the fading light of Motown's golden era. The Jackson Five saw their first four singles go to number one in the US in 1970, an unprecedented feat. His singing on 'I Want You Back', 'ABC', 'The Love You Save' and 'I'll Be There' showed phrasing and expression astonishing in one so young. Solo hits followed through the late Seventies but it was the album *Thriller* and the singles taken from it like 'Beat It' and 'Billie Jean' that put his career into orbit. *Thriller* became the best-selling album of all time with sales of 35 million and counting.

Jackson fashioned a highly danceable pop/soul hybrid featuring pumping rhythms and an increasingly mannered vocal style. His knee-jerk tendency to attach a gasp to the end of every line only evoked the picture of a small crowd of agile gnomes sticking pins in his legs during the recording. The cod-Gothic 'Monster Mash' imagery, backed up by a voice-over from Vincent Price, meant *Thriller* was promoted with a 14-minute video which generated more interest than the song itself. This video helped to open the previously rock-oriented MTV to black music.

(Rap see block lyric)

Verse 2:
You hear the door slam
And realize there's nowhere left to run
You feel the cold hand
And wonder if you'll ever see the sun
You close your eyes
And hope that this is just imagination
But all the while
You hear the creature creepin' up behind
You're out of time.

'Cause this is thriller, thriller night
There ain't no second chance
Against the thing with forty eyes
You know, it's thriller, thriller night
You're fighting for your life
Inside a killer thriller tonight.

Verse 3:
They're out to get you
There's demons closin' in on ev'ry side
They will posess you
Unless you change that number on your dial
Now is the time
For you and I to cuddle close together
All thru the night
I'll save you from the terror on the screen
I'll make you see.

That this is thriller, thriller night
'Cause I could thrill you more
Than any ghost would dare to try
Girl, this is thriller, thriller night
So let me hold you tight
And share a killer thriller.

Rap:
Darkness falls across the land
The midnight hour is close at hand
Creatures crawl in search of blood
To terrorize y 'awl's neighborhood
And whosoever shall be found
Without the soul forgetting down
Must stand and face the hounds of hell
And rot inside a corpse's shell.

The foulest stench is in the air
The funk of forty thousand years
And grizzly ghouls from every tomb
Are closing in to seal your doom
And though you fight to stay alive
Your body starts to shiver
For no mere mortal can resist
The evil of a thriller.

I Just Called To Say I Love You

Stevie Wonder
1984 – UK: 1, US: 1

Starting with 'Fingertips Part 2' (US: 1, 1963) when he was only thirteen, Wonder spent the Sixties at Motown racking up hits like 'My Cherie Amour', 'I Was Made To Love Her', 'For Once In My Life' and 'Signed, Sealed, Delivered'. In the early Seventies he gained unparalleled artistic control over his career, releasing albums like *Talking Book*, *Innervisions* and *Songs In The Key Of Life*.

His hits have continued to the present day, thanks to the evergreen vivacity and remarkable optimism that informs Wonder's music.

Inevitably, his two biggest hits lack the invention and harder edge of 'Heaven Help Us All' or 'Superstition'. 'Ebony And Ivory', co-written with Paul McCartney, gave him the biggest hit of his career in 1982. The (unusual for him) downbeat 'I Just Called...' offers the spectacle of a singer who once recorded with one of the all-time great rhythm sections (Motown's Funk Brothers) in sync with a drum-machine.

The nasal tone and vocal decorations in evidence were hugely influential. Featured in *The Woman In Red*, 'I Just Called... ' won a Best Song Oscar. Astonishingly, this was Motown's biggest-seller in the UK.

One of the greatest mutual admiration societies of politics in the century, Maggie and Ronnie in their heydays.

I Just Called To Say I Love You

Words & Music by Stevie Wonder

Verse 2:
No April rain, no flowers bloom
No wedding Saturday within the month of June
But what it is, is something true
Made up of these three words that I must say to you.

Verse 3:
No summer's high; no warm July
No harvest moon to light one tender August night.
No autumn breeze; no falling leaves
Not even time for birds to fly to southern skies.

Verse 4:
No Libra sun; no Halloween
No giving thanks to all the Christmas joy you bring.
But what it is, though old so new
To fill your heart like no three words could ever do.

Careless Whisper

Words & Music by George Michael & Andrew Ridgeley

Slowly

1. I feel so— un-sure— as I take your hand— and lead you to the dance floor;
(Verses 2 & 3 see block lyrics)

as the mu-sic dies— some-thing in your eyes— calls to mind a sil-ver screen— and you're its sad good-bye.

— I'm nev-er gon-na dance a-gain, guil-ty feet have got— no rhy-thm, though it's ea-sy to pre-tend, I

know you're not— a fool.— I should have known bet-ter than to cheat a friend, and

waste a chance that I've— been gi-ven, so I'm nev-er gon-na dance a-gain— the way I dance— with you.

way I dance-with you, oh.—

way I dance— with you.—

Verse 2:
Time can never mend
The careless whisper of a good friend
To the heart and mind
Ignorance is kind
There's no comfort in the truth
Pain is all you'll find.

Verse 3:
Tonight the music seems so loud
I wish that we could lose this crowd
Maybe it's better this way
If we'd hurt each other with the things we want to say
We could have been so good together
We could have lived this dance forever
But now who's gonna dance with me? Please dance.

*George Michael and
Andrew Ridgeley...Wham!
'Careless Whisper' saw
the end of the group and
the start of Michael's
superstardom.*

Careless Whisper
*Wham! / George Michael
1984: UK: 1; US: 1*
'Careless Whisper' signalled the
approaching end of Wham!, the
duo George Michael formed
with the under-employed
Andrew Ridgeley, and the
beginning of Michael's career as
one of the most successful and
career-minded solo singers of
the Eighties.

Michael put out 'I Want Your

Sex', 'Faith' and an album *Listen
Without Prejudice*, and eventually
broke through into a new and
wider commercial acceptance as
the Phil Collins of the Nineties.
'Careless Whisper' is a ruthlessly
executed, laser-guided
smoocher, complete with the
most ear-pricking sax intro since
'Baker Street'. Released in the
UK as a solo record but in the
US as Wham!

For much of his career

George Michael was known
as the ultimate control-freak,
seeking to personally direct
every aspect of his career with
meticulous care. His much
publicised indiscretion in a
Los Angeles park led him to
his 'coming out' as a bisexual,
a gesture that seems to have
done his popularity no harm
whatsoever. Honesty is evidently
still a valued commodity in pop,
even in the cynical Nineties.

Against All Odds

Phil Collins
1984 – US: 1; UK: 2

Phil Collins' huge success as a
solo artist in the Eighties was
resented by rock critics who
thought he should have stayed
on the drum stool in Genesis.
But the same critics didn't like
Genesis anyway. It was a big
step from the progressive rock
of *The Lamb Lies Down On
Broadway* to the populist appeal
of 'Missed Again' and 'You
Can't Hurry Love'. Thought an
unlikely front-man, Collins was
recognised as not only a fine
drummer but a good songwriter
and an idiosyncratic singer.

'Against All Odds' was
included on the *Face Value*
album and in a Jeff Bridges' film
of the same name. It's a
powerful piano/strings ballad,
with one of Collins' patented
drum intros, a trick first used on
'In The Air Tonight' which
caused many an ornament to
tumble off the nation's
mantelpieces. The lyric deals
with the regret of the
abandoned lover. Collins lifts
his singing for the last two
choruses, unexpectedly
demonstrative on the words
'left', 'there's', 'wait' and the last
'I'll still be standing'. It's an
utterly committed vocal,
without a trace of self-conscious
'over-souling' and he
commendably resists the big
finish. The song's unpredictable
route to the key chord adds a
flicker of hope: you may not get
what you want, but you might
get what you need.

*July 13, 1985: Live Aid,
Wembley Stadium, London.*

*Following pages
The front rows of the
Royal Box at Live Aid…
the Thin White Duke,
the Princess, two Queens,
the Prince and a Knight to be.*

Against All Odds (Take A Look At Me Now)

Words & Music by Phil Collins

Slow rock

1. How can I just let you walk a-way, just let you leave with-out a trace? When I
(Verses 2 & 3 see block lyric)
stand here tak- ing ev- 'ry breath with you ooh. You're the
on- ly one who real- ly knew me at all.

2, 3. So take a look at me now, well there's just an emp-ty space, and there's no-thing
left here to re- mind me, just the mem- 'ry of your face. Well take a look at me now,
well there's just an emp-ty space, and you com-in' back
to me is a-gainst the odds, and that's what I've got to face.

D.C. 2. 3. I — I've got to face. Take a good look at me now, — I've got to take.
Take a look at me now.

Verse 2:
How can you just walk away from me
When all I can do is watch you leave?
'Cause we shared the laughter and the pain
And even shared the tears.
You're the only one who really knew me at all.

Verse 3:
I wish I could just make you turn around
Turn around and see me cry.
There's so much I need to say to you
So many reasons why.
You're the only one who really knew me at all.

(Everything I Do) I Do It For You

Words by Bryan Adams & Robert John 'Mutt' Lange
Music by Michael Kamen

Verse 2:

Look into your heart
You will find there's nothin' there to hide.
Take me as I am, take my life
I would give it all, I would sacrifice.

Don't tell me it's not worth fighting for
I can't help it, there's nothin' I want more.
You know it's true, everything I do
I do it for you.

(Everything I Do)
I Do It For You
Bryan Adams
1991 – UK: 1; US: 1

As record-buyers were
gradually alienated from pop by
its increasing mechanisation
and banality, the average stay of
a single in the UK Top Forty
became shorter and shorter. It
was amazing therefore that this
song stayed at number one for a
record-breaking 16 weeks. By
1991 only 16 songs had spent
eight or more consecutive weeks
at number one since 1952. How
did Bryan Adams, who'd
previously hit with rockers like
'Somebody' and 'Run To You',
manage it?

'Everything I Do' was the
theme tune to a successful film
(*Robin Hood, Prince Of Thieves*), a
love song with not rose but
green-tinted spectacles. In its
video Merrie Olde Englande
collided with Stratocaster
guitars, and the message was
that the Age of Chivalry was not
dead. 'Everything I Do' wasted
nothing through 64 elegant bars
of platinum craftsmanship. It
was a slow ballad, but not
depressingly so; it had a gravelly
vocal that suggested there might
be an outburst but there wasn't;
it had a short guitar solo and a
few rock trimmings but nothing
to rattle the jewellery too much.
It had a nice coda with a
temporary swoon onto F minor
and a poignant penultimate
minor chord where you weren't
expecting one.

*An East Berlin border
guard is given a rose by a
West Berliner in late
1989. Within hours the
Berlin Wall was breached.*

Tears In Heaven

Eric Clapton

1992 – UK: 5; US: 2

Eric Clapton's life has been a tempestuous one, full of reversals of fortune and wounds (some self-inflicted, some not) which have inspired his music. 'Tears In Heaven' originated in the tragic death of Clapton's young son Conor, who fell from a window in a Manhattan apartment. It was released as part of his hugely successful *Unplugged* MTV set.

It's executed on two acoustic guitars with a little bass and percussion, and there's no guitar hero flourishes.

Hardly an easy subject to write about, the subject-matter is highly charged but with the sure touch of a mature artist Clapton deliberately underplays the Will Jennings' lyric. Sometimes less is more, especially in the case of songs about the death of a child. Structurally the song has some interesting touches, notably the step-wise descending sequence in the latter part of the verse and the brief letting in of the light when the key changes to C major in the middle eight. Given the personal nature of 'Tears In Heaven', it's difficult to imagine many wanting to cover this – it would feel too much like an act of emotional trespass.

The end result has an un-expected, quiet dignity. Pop music is rarely this elegiac and as tasteful at the same time.

The view of the Earth from the Russian space station Mir. Launched in 1986, it became the longest used manned space vehicle. Over 100 astronauts from many nations worked aboard Mir before it was eventually abandoned on August 27, 1999.

Tears In Heaven

Words & Music by Eric Clapton & Will Jennings

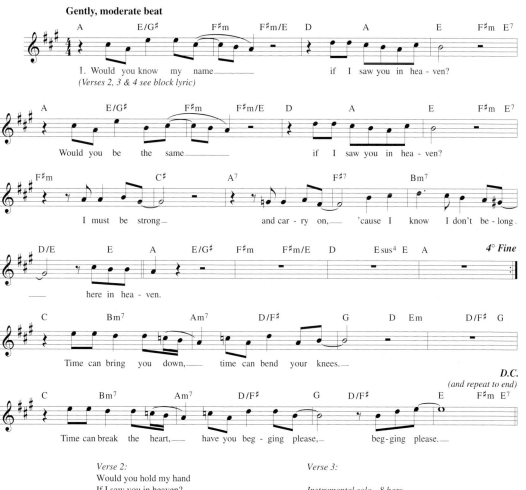

Gently, moderate beat

A   E/G♯   F♯m   F♯m/E   D   A   E   F♯m   E⁷

1. Would you know my name_____ if I saw you in hea - ven?
(Verses 2, 3 & 4 see block lyric)

A   E/G♯   F♯m   F♯m/E   D   A   E   F♯m   E⁷

Would you be the same_____ if I saw you in hea - ven?

F♯m   C♯   A⁷   F♯⁷   Bm⁷

I must be strong__ and car - ry on,__ 'cause I know I don't be - long__

D/E   E   A   E/G♯   F♯m   F♯m/E   D   Esus⁴ E A   *4° Fine*

__ here in hea - ven.

C   Bm⁷   Am⁷   D/F♯   G   D   Em   D/F♯   G

Time can bring you down,__ time can bend your knees.__

D.C.
(and repeat to end)

C   Bm⁷   Am⁷   D/F♯   G   D/F♯   E   F♯m   E⁷

Time can break the heart, have you beg - ging please,__ beg - ging please.

Verse 2:
Would you hold my hand
If I saw you in heaven?
Would you help me stand
If I saw you in heaven?
I'll find my way
Through night and day
'Cause I know I just can't stay
Here in heaven.

Verse 3:

Instrumental solo - 8 bars

Beyond the door
There's peace, I'm sure
And I know there'll be no more
Tears in heaven.

Verse 4:
Would you know my name
If I saw you in heaven?
Would you be the same
If I saw you in heaven?
I must be strong
And carry on
'Cause I know I don't belong
Here in heaven.

Have I Told You Lately?

Words & Music by Van Morrison

Verse 2:
Oh the morning sun in all its glory
Greets the day with hope and comfort too
And you fill my life with laughter
You can make it better
Ease my troubles that what you do.

Have I Told You Lately?
Rod Stewart
1993 – UK: 5; US: 5
Despite a string of successful albums through the Eighties Rod Stewart's career never quite shook off the memory of the artistic credibility and critical claim of his wonderful pre-*Atlantic Crossing* English-based recordings. For much of this time he seemed unable to comprehend why his earlier music was held in such high esteem. Perhaps it was the declining health of one-time fellow Face Ronnie Lane that turned Stewart's thoughts back to his glory years, but MTV's popular *Unplugged* programmes offered an opportunity to re-visit those songs. For added authenticity Stewart invited Ronnie Wood to play some of the guitar parts. The resulting *Unplugged ... And Seated* set of 1993 was well-received and spawned several singles.

'Have I Told You Lately?' is a Van Morrison tune which originated on *Avalon Sunset* (1989). It's a slow ballad with predictable rhymes and a pretty acoustic guitar break which stands happily alongside Stewart's best early songs. With Stewart's voice a little threadbare, the emotion is intensified, and it was guaranteed to appeal to a wide audience. Van Morrison's version is altogether more dignified and romantic.

Wonderwall

Oasis

1995 – UK: 2; US: 8

In the mid-Nineties Brit-pop was born. Oasis wanted to be the New Beatles and Blur the New Small Faces. 'Wonderwall' almost reached the top when Oasis released their mega-selling LP (*What's The Story*) *Morning Glory?* fascinating a generation that had never realised that a good song might a) feature acoustic guitars and a cello, and b) no drum machine.

Named after a Sixties soundtrack by George Harrison, 'Wonderwall' is a love song of sorts based on a cycle of four easy chords for the intro. Even beginners could fumble through it. Acoustic guitar sales rocketed and 'Wonderwall' became a music-shop anthem. Noel put together a dignified lyric with a touch of romantic sentiment that was unusual for the macho image that Oasis liked to portray. Indeed, the opening line – "Today is gonna be the day…" – has now become as memorable as anything in the Oasis catalogue.

The unsung hero of 'Wonderwall' is drummer Alan White whose fine brush work before the last verse lifts the song immeasurably. 'Wonderwall' has become a classic Oasis song, though many fans prefer 'Cast No Shadow' from the same album.

Liam and Noel Gallagher of Oasis, a major force behind the Brit Pop of the late Nineties. By the summer of 1999 the two brothers were the only surviving members, their three fellow band members had all departed; the pressures of Oasis' huge and sudden success was blamed.

Wonderwall

Words & Music by Noel Gallagher

Verse 2:

Back beat, the word is on the street
That the fire in your heart is out
I'm sure you've heard it all before
But you never really had a doubt.
I don't believe that anybody
Feels the way I do about you now.

And all the roads we have to walk are winding
And all the lights that lead us there are blinding
There are many things that I would like to say to you
But I don't know how.

Say You'll Be There

Words & Music by Eliot Kennedy, Jon B, Victoria Aadams,
Melanie Brown, Emma Bunton, Melanie Chisholm & Geri Halliwell

Moderately

1. Last time that we had this con-ver-sa-tion I de-ci-ded we should be friends, yeah.

But now we're go-ing round in cir-cles, tell me will this de-ja vu ne-ver end. Oh

The morning after the election before. The Blair family on the doorstep of 10 Downing Street.

Say You'll Be There

The Spice Girls
1996 – UK: 1

The Spice Girls arrived on the British pop scene with the energy of the national grid. Like so many other teen bands before them, they were packaged by a marketing genius but The Spice Girls were somehow different. Firstly, they were girls; secondly, they at least seemed to have some ideas of their own; thirdly, they hung on to their earnings. While their revolutionary zeal lacked the depth of, say, The Slits, they at least opened the doors to like-minded females. What was remarkable about their success was the age of their fans – girls as young as six or seven were drawn into pop for the first time, and primary school playgrounds throughout the land echoed to the sound of little girls singing The Spice Girls' hits while they did their best to imitate their dance routines.

The Spice Girls themselves boasted Disneyesque names – Posh, Ginger, Baby, Sporty and Scarey – and a suitably right-on message: Girl Power. 'Say You'll Be There' was one of many hits, a slowish dance tune, with a few harmonies, a bit of souling on the outro, a Wonder-type harmonica break and a bridge not unlike one of Madonna's hits.

Naysayers suggested that when Geri 'Ginger Spice' left, the group was doomed but in the event they became even more successful, making an enjoyable pop film and taking America by storm, a feat generally elusive to teen bands. As the century ends the remaining Spices are ubiquitous celebrities, beloved of the tabloid press, especially Victoria 'Posh' Aadams who married high profile footballer David Beckham.

Verse 2:
If you put two and two together you will see what our friendship is for
If you can't work this equation then I guess I'll have to show you the door.
There is no need to say you love me, it would be better left unsaid.

I'm giving you everything, all that joy can bring, this I swear
And all that I want from you, is a promise you will be there.
Yeah I want you.

Verse 3: (Instrumental)
Any fool can see they're falling, gotta make you understand.
To Coda

Daily Mail

THURSDAY, AUGUST 12, 1999   NATIONAL NEWSPAPER OF THE YEAR 35p

ECLIPSE
SPECIAL
EDITION

AWESOME

The light fantastic: As the moon covers the sun, the solar corona radiates across the heavens in an awe-inspiring halo moment of total eclipse that brought Britain to a standstill yesterday as millions saw day turn to night   FULL STORY: PAGE

INSIDE: Weather 2, Waterhouse 14, Dempster 33, Femail 35-45, Letters 46, TV 47-50, Coffee Break 57-59, City 60-62, Sport 63-72

ECLIPSE RD E13

My Heart Will Go On

Celine Dion
1998 – UK: 1; US

With Whitney Houston and Mariah Carey, Celine Dion is one of the most successful female Nineties MOR singers, carving out a career by positioning herself in the market with a veneer of French sophistication and polish. She was tailor-made for delivering this power-ballad, the theme tune to the most successful film ever. James Cameron's three-hour epic *Titanic* focused on the sudden but star-crossed love between below decks hero Leonardo DiCaprio and posh heroine Kate Winslett. Having

inspired a change for the good in her, he dies in the water, but she Makes It and goes on to Another Life. Thus, 'My Heart Will Go On' is played as the credits roll.

Along with The Corrs, this record established the new international musical language of the heart of commercially produced Celticisms, courtesy of the Irish pipes. For the millions who bought this cleverly orchestrated ballad, with its twinkly harp, slow beat and modulated finale, the film's imagery and its music are one.

August, 1999:
In the last months of the century, the total eclipse of the sun was a-once-in-a-lifetime natural spectacle, watched by millions across Europe and the Middle East.

My Heart Will Go On
(Love Theme from *Titanic*)

Words by Will Jennings
Music by James Horner

Verse 2:
Love can touch us one time
And last for a lifetime
And never let go till we're one.
Love was when I loved you
One true time I hold to
In my life we'll always go on.

4/03 (47264)